Euripides' *Medea*

This book offers a new, accurate and actable translation of one of Euripides' most popular plays, together with a commentary which provides insight into the challenges it sets for production and suggestions for how to solve them.

The introduction discusses the social and cultural context of the play and its likely impact on the original audience, the way in which it was originally performed, the challenges which the lead roles present today and *Medea's* implications for the modern audience. The text of the translation is followed by the 'Theatrical Commentary' section on the issues involved in staging each scene and chorus today, embodying insights gained from a professional production. Notes on the translation, a glossary of names, suggestions for further reading and a chronology of Euripides' life and times round out the volume.

The book is intended for use by theatre practitioners who wish to stage or workshop *Medea* and by students both of drama, theatre and performance and of classical studies.

Michael Ewans is Conjoint Professor of Drama in the School of Humanities, Creative Industries and Social Science at the University of Newcastle, Australia. His 11 books include two volumes each of translations of plays by Aeschylus, Sophocles and Aristophanes, all with theatrical commentaries.

'Michael Ewans has produced . . . an elegant, thoughtful, careful, and moving text of Euripides' *Medea* . . . [and] a splendid analysis of the play that will make it much, much easier for those who wish to create a production of this important and challenging play . . . Ewans discusses the various challenges and how these challenges can be dealt with by contemporary practitioners. . . . Ewans' excellent work deserves to be read, considered, and brought to life in theaters everywhere.'

Mary-Kay Gamel, *University of California Santa Cruz, USA*

Euripides' *Medea*

Translation and Theatrical
Commentary

Michael Ewans

Routledge
Taylor & Francis Group

LONDON AND NEW YORK

Cover image: Claudia Bedford as Medea at 1242ff, in Michael Ewans' 2021 production. © Jo Roberts. Reproduced with permission

First published 2022
by Routledge
2 Park Square, Milton Park, Abingdon, Oxon OX14 4RN

and by Routledge
605 Third Avenue, New York, NY 10158

Routledge is an imprint of the Taylor & Francis Group, an informa business

© 2022 Michael Ewans

British Library Cataloguing-in-Publication Data
A catalogue record for this book is available from the British Library

Library of Congress Cataloging-in-Publication Data
Names: Ewans, Michael, 1946– author. | Euripides. Medea. English (Ewans)
Title: Euripides' *Medea*: translation and theatrical commentary/Michael Ewans.
Description: Abingdon, Oxon: Routledge, 2022. | Includes bibliographical references and index.
Identifiers: LCCN 2021037087 (print) | LCCN 2021037088 (ebook)
Subjects: LCSH: Euripides. Medea. | Euripides—Dramatic production.
Classification: LCC PA3985 .E93 2022 (print) | LCC PA3985 (ebook) | DDC 882/.01—dc23
LC record available at https://lccn.loc.gov/2021037087
LC ebook record available at https://lccn.loc.gov/2021037088

ISBN: 978-1-032-10545-1 (hbk)
ISBN: 978-1-032-10543-7 (pbk)
ISBN: 978-1-003-21584-4 (ebk)

DOI: 10.4324/9781003215844

Typeset in Times New Roman
by Apex CoVantage, LLC

Contents

Figure

Preface

Like my previous translations of Aeschylus, Sophocles and Aristophanes, this English version of *Medea* is designed to be both accurate and actable. Like them also, it is followed by a 'Theatrical Commentary' – but with an important difference. All but one of my previous productions were performed in a replica of the original Greek theatre shape, with the audience surrounding the action on three sides. But theatres with this configuration are rare (we had to use a bare-space Drama Studio and install raked seating, though for Sophocles' *Aias* and *Electra* we were able to perform in a natural outdoor amphitheatre). *Medea* by contrast was performed in a normal modern theatre with an end-on audience, and it was fascinating to investigate through a research production how the play, written for performance in a very different theatre, could be adapted to work effectively in this much smaller performance space. The 'Theatrical Commentary' reflects our findings.

I owe thanks to Graham Ley, Marguerite Johnson, Carl Caulfield and Mary-Kay Gamel for reading and commenting on drafts of this book and above all to the cast and crew of the premiere production, who taught me so much about the play and ways of staging it today.

Michael Ewans
The University of Newcastle, Australia

Chronology

Chronology of Euripides' life	Chronology of Euripides' times
Born c. 485–80	
	456 Death of Aeschylus
455 Enters tragedy contest for the first time	
	449 Peace of Callias ends hostilities with Persia
	443 Pericles becomes Athens' leading politician
441 First victory in the competition	441 Samos revolts from the Athenian empire
	439/8 Pericles puts down the revolt in Samos
438 Second with four dramas, including *Alcestis*, his first surviving play	438 Sophocles wins tragedy contest, probably with *Antigone*
	432 Athenian alliance with Corcyra
431 Third with four dramas, including *Medea*	431 The Peloponnesians invade Attica; start of the Peloponnesian War
c. 430 *Children of Heracles*	430 Outbreak of the great plague at Athens. Sophocles, *Women of Trachis* (?)
429 *Hippolytus* (first version, not performed)	429 Death of Pericles
428 *Hippolytus* (second version; won first prize)	
c. 425 *Andromache*	425 Cleon becomes Athens' leading politician Aristophanes, *Acharnians* (his first surviving comedy) Sophocles, *Oedipus the King* (?)
c. 424 *Hecuba*	424 Aristophanes, *Knights*
c. 423 *Suppliant Women*	
	422 Aristophanes, *Wasps*
	421 Aristophanes, *Peace*. Peace of Nicias between Athens and Sparta

c. 420 *Electra*	420 Alliance between Athens and Argos
c. 418 *Heracles*	
	416 Athenians sack Melos
415 Trojan tetralogy, including	415 Athenian expedition to Sicily
Women of Troy	
c. 414–3 *Iphigenia among the*	414 Spartans resume hostilities against
Taurians, Ion	Athens
412 *Helen* and the lost *Andromeda*	
411–9 *Phoenician Women*	411 (January) Aristophanes: *Lysistrata*
	(March) Aristophanes: *The Women's*
	Festival
	(May) right-wing coup at Athens;
	government of 'The Four Hundred'
	(August) 'Four Hundred' expelled
	and replaced by a moderate
	oligarchy of 'The Five Thousand'
	410 Full democracy restored at Athens
	409 Sophocles, *Philoctetes*
408 *Orestes*	
408/7 Perhaps departs from	
Athens for the court of	
Archelaus in Macedonia	
407/6 Dies, leaving *Bacchae* and	
Iphigenia at Aulis	
	406 Death of Sophocles
405 *Bacchae* and *Iphigenia at*	405 Aristophanes, *Frogs*
Aulis win first prize	Final defeat of Athens at
	Aegospotami
	404 Surrender of Athens and installation
	of a Spartan-backed junta, 'The
	Thirty'
	403 Restoration of democracy and
	general amnesty
The date of the satyr-play *Cyclops*	
is unknown	

Introduction

1 *Medea* and Greek values

At the Festival of Dionysus in Athens in 431 BCE, Euripides exhibited four dramas, including *Medea*, for which he was awarded the third prize, placed last after Aeschylus' son Euphorion (who may have been reviving one of his father's tetralogies) and Sophocles. It is possible that his other two tragedies that year (*Philoctetes* and *Dictys*) and the satyr-play *Theristai* were of poor quality or that the material (like *Medea*) was controversial. It is however probable that *Medea* offended the sensibilities of the Athenian audience; in this tragedy, which Euripides presented first in his set, he unfolded with great clarity and power a story that was deeply disturbing to them.

Euripides chose not to dramatize the heroic quest of the Argonauts to bring back the Golden Fleece from Colchis, nor the romantic blossoming of love between Jason and Medea and the ways in which she enabled him to achieve the goal of his quest; instead, he focused on the sordid aftermath of their return to Greece, after Medea had killed her brother to make their escape from Colchis possible. When Jason and Medea were accused of murdering his uncle Pelias, in his native city of Iolcus in Thessaly, they sought refuge at Corinth and had two sons. Euripides focused his tragedy on the consequences of Jason's recent decision to secure his and his children's future at Corinth by rejecting Medea and marrying King Creon's daughter. Medea took revenge on Jason both by contriving the deaths of Creon and his daughter (as in other versions of the legend) and – in a shocking, probably new variant – by murdering her two sons, after which she escaped from Corinth to take refuge in Athens in a chariot provided by her grandfather, the Sun God.[1]

Medea begins the drama as an underdog; she is a woman – only one place above a slave in the hierarchy of ancient Greek society – and an unmarried mother (Medea and Jason had no marriage ceremony valid in Greece). She is also an exile and a foreigner ('barbarian') – though only

DOI: 10.4324/9781003215844-1

Jason emphasizes this (536ff., 1330ff.). In all these ways, she is marked out from the ruling class, which consisted in contemporary Athens only of the ethnically Greek male citizens. Euripides first presents Medea as heart-broken, suicidal and grief-stricken by having been so unceremoniously and brutally abandoned. The Nurse's opening statement invites us to view what has happened in three ways: (1) in the household of Medea (before whose doors the action is set), 'all's enmity; the closest bonds are now diseased' (16); (2) Jason has betrayed Medea and his sons by sleeping with the prin-cess (17–18); (3) Medea is wretched because she has been deprived of *timē* ('had her honour stripped away', 20; cf. 33). *Timē* was a powerful word and a strange one to use repeatedly about a woman since *timē* – honour and sta-tus, measured by a person's actual situation and possessions – was normally a central component of Greek *male* excellence.

The 'disease' that is poisoning the household spreads as the action unfolds until both Jason's old and new family are destroyed at the end. It has been caused entirely by Jason's infidelity; Euripides consistently emphasizes the importance for a woman of fair treatment as a sexual being (265–6, 569–71, 1290ff.), and in the Finale, Jason bitterly accuses Medea of causing all this destruction just because of her sexual feelings, to which she replies fiercely, 'D'you think that is a small affliction for a woman?' (1366–8). It is also repeatedly stressed that Jason has broken the oaths to remain faithful to Medea, which he swore by the gods in Colchis (21ff., 439, 492ff., 778).

In consequence, Euripides can appeal for sympathy for Medea in her opening speech on the lot of women (230ff.) and through the sympathy of the Corinthian Women – especially in Choros 2 (410ff.). And she is imaged firmly, despite her foreign origins, as a normal upper-class female by the early reference (30; cf. 923) to her 'white skin' (high-born Greek women were not supposed to expose themselves much to the sun).

However, the drama rapidly moves on into new, deeply disturbing ter-ritory. Images of Medea as like a wild beast (92–3, 188), coupled with the Nurse's fears for the children (36ff., 98ff., 116ff.), have already hinted that Medea is more than the weeping 'female-as-victim' that she at first appears to be. And in her speech about the mistreatment of women, Medea uttered the infamous lines:

> I'd rather stand three times
> With shield in hand than give birth once.
>
> (250–1)

This was a direct assault on the view, fundamental to Greek values, that males are superior to females because their fighting ability and heroism protect the household and the city.

Worse was to come. The idea that Medea has been dishonoured by Jason's betrayal continues to be stressed in the early scenes (after 20 and 33 cf. 255, 314, and 438). And she is now entirely alone since as her brother's murderer she has no paternal house to which she can return, accepting her divorce passively, like a normal Greek woman (358ff., 502ff., 603, 710ff.). Medea makes a surprising response to this situation; like a normal Greek *male* of noble birth, she refuses to allow herself to be shamed or her enemies to be able to laugh at her and resolves to take revenge on those who have diminished her *timē* (367ff.). Her reason is simple – and again normal for a Greek noble *man*; as a descendant of the Sun God, she is better born than her enemy since the princess, who has replaced her in Jason's bed, is a descendant of the infamous Sisyphus (383, 403ff.).

Greek male ethics were simple; *aretē* (excellence) consisted in helping your friends (especially your relatives) and harming your enemies; help and harm were equally important. And these were not merely the ethics of the larger-than-life-size heroes of Greek epic and tragedy, like Homer's Achilles and Sophocles' Aias (Ajax);[2] they were the values of the ordinary man in the street in the mid to late fifth century.[3]

Medea harnesses male revenge ethics to a wrong done to her womanhood and female sexuality, and she obtains her revenge because she is more intelligent and cleverer than either Creon or Jason. She successfully fawns on Creon enough to gain the extra day that she needs to destroy his daughter (367ff.; cf. 407–9), and in her second scene with Jason, she persuades him of her feigned submission. She does this both by the care with which she uses language in her speech at 869ff. and by appealing to Jason's stereotype of women as prone to overemotional immediate reactions (889ff.). Jason is totally deceived. He patronizingly tells Medea that her initial fury was quite natural in the circumstances, and he is delighted that she has become a 'sensible' woman (908ff.) – using the word *sōphrōn*, by which Greek males commended prudence and passivity in their females. Medea can now use poison against the princess and the king; she has already secured a safe refuge in Athens from King Aegeus (who has made a surprise appearance, visiting her for advice in the middle of the drama). She also knows (though Euripides does not let her mention this, so as not to spoil the *coup de théâtre* of the Finale) that she has the Sun God's flying chariot at her disposal. So we discover that she has placed herself in a position where she can destroy them both and escape from Corinth unscathed.

However, Medea's plan for the murders demands that she send her children to give the princess a poisoned robe – and (in an echo of the traditional version of the story) this could clearly lead to their being killed in vengeance by Creon's relatives. That is intolerable – again because it is unbearable to be laughed at by enemies. She will not permit it to happen; she will kill her own children (791ff.; cf. 1237–41). This goes against the revenge code; she will be harming her friends in order to harm her enemies.

At this point, the audience realizes that Medea's gender exacts a hideous price for her adoption of male values; because she is female and emotionally attached to her sons, her revenge must cause her great grief since she can only achieve it through their agency. Euripides develops her agonizing dilemma; if she does not want to be considered worthless and weak, how can she avenge herself on her enemies, and punish Jason the oath-breaker, without hurting her dearest ones?

When the children have delivered the poisoned robe and crown to Jason's bride, they return with permission to remain at Corinth. Euripides then dramatizes the absolute misery of a woman who has born and raised children for nothing (1021ff.). When the boys look intently at her and smile (1040ff.), Medea for a moment abandons her plan to murder them, but she strengthens her resolve, returning to the need not to become laughed at by her enemies (1049–55). There are difficulties in the remainder of her speech – enough for some scholars to delete the whole of 1056–80 as a later actor's interpolation to increase the pathos of the monologue.[4] I believe that all these lines except 1056–63 are genuine;[5] the spectators saw a terrible battle between Medea's desire for revenge and her womanly need to let her children live. In the end, she acknowledges that what she intends to do is utterly wrong:

> But anger has control over my plans –
> Anger, which is the greatest cause of human pain.
> (1079–80)[6]

And Medea's final exit speech, just before she goes into her house to murder the children, is of even greater power and pathos:

> Arm yourself, my heart; why do I delay
> committing this awful but necessary crime?
> Come, desperate hand, take up the sword,
> take it, and creep to where the misery of life begins.
> Don't weaken; don't remember your children,
> how they are very dear, how you gave birth to them, but just
> for this short day forget your sons; then
> you can lament them. Even though you kill them,
> they were born dear to you. I am unfortunate.
> (1242ff.)

Euripides' Medea began the drama lamenting because, as a woman in a male-dominated society, she has been treated little better than a slave. At the end she has triumphed over her enemies, and, although she has suffered great grief herself, she has given much more suffering to Jason, who is now forced to adopt the normally female role of grieving impotently for lost relatives. Jason is unheard and desperate as he abuses her and calls upon the gods (1389ff., 1460ff.). Medea escapes unscathed after her revenge and even denies Jason the chance to bury their children – that she will do herself (1378ff.).

A little over 80 years ago, one editor sought to detach the sympathetic portrayal of Medea's emotions in the first half of the drama from the horror of this revenge; 'the fantastic conclusion . . . – child-murder, dragon-chariot – is an end and not an answer. This is no longer a part of life, but of myth and magic – no longer about a woman, but about a barbarian sorceress'.[7] It is still important to oppose this position today and insist that Euripides conducts the drama of Medea's decision to murder the children on the same plane of reality as the earlier action. As already noted, there is nothing barbarian about Euripides' Medea except her birthplace; more importantly, in view of the direction that most treatments of the legend were to take after Euripides, his Medea is not a 'barbarian sorceress' – though she has practised magic in Colchis and Iolcus.[8] (She is a witch and a megalomaniac sorceress in Ovid's *Metamorphoses* and in Seneca's tragedy *Medea*, which was highly influential in the reception of the Medea story during and after the Renaissance.)[9] What changes towards the end of the drama is not the reality of Medea but the perspective from which the Athenian audience was made to view her. When the tragedy begins, she is a woman (though an exceptional one, as a former princess and a possessor of magical powers) – below the males in status; next, she shows herself their equal by adopting their revenge code and then their superior when she achieves her vengeance on the man who has wronged her. Finally, she ends the drama like a goddess – appearing on high, dispensing matters in accordance with her will, prophesying the future and instituting a cult, just as gods do in later fifth-century tragedies.

In Greek ethics, there was no credible way of criticizing what we might think to be an excessive revenge; provided you were successful, the fullest possible revenge on an enemy who had wronged you was justifiable and indeed essential. Nor could a character be censured for gloating over a fallen enemy, as Medea does over the horrible death of Jason's bride at 1125 and 1135. This is why Euripides' strategy in *Medea* was so devastating. In the second half of this tragedy, Euripides obliged the men in his audience to sit and watch how a woman with a just cause uses normal female tactics (poison) to triumph over men – and they could not simply brush this triumph aside as the revolting act of a barbarian, as Jason tries to do (1339: 'no Greek woman would have dared to do this'); infanticide by mothers was a feature both of Greek myth and of contemporary Greek life.[10] When Medea avenges herself on Creon, the princess and Jason, her total success and scot-free escape left a normal Athenian male with no valid grounds in his ethical system on which to detest her – as one of the Women of Corinth rightly comments after the deaths of Creon and his daughter: 'It seems that on this day the god/ has imposed many sufferings on Jason – and justly so' (1231–2), but the spectacle of a foreign, immigrant woman succeeding so totally in her revenge against a Greek man, who was only divorcing her, as many Greek men did to older wives, would make them very uneasy. (Technically Jason was not divorcing Medea, as they had not undergone a marriage ceremony. But the oaths by the gods which he took in Colchis to remain faithful to her were much more powerful and binding than a formal Greek marriage.) The males in the audience could not condemn Medea at the end, as they would undoubtedly want to, because they could not deny that she possesses what mattered in their value system – power and success.

The reaction which Euripides forced from female members of his audience was almost equally drastic.[11] Medea vigorously denounces the inequity of a woman's lot in ancient Greece; she asserts the worth of women, and she implies – and the Corinthian Women state openly – that some females possess intelligence equal to, sometimes superior to, that of many men (1081ff.). All this was bound to elicit strong approval from most women. Medea then uses her cunning and intelligence to avenge herself for a wrong done to her womanhood – but in doing so she must destroy one of the most fundamental aspects of being female, the bond between mother and children. So the women were first encouraged to admire Medea – but then she does something which would naturally inspire their complete revulsion. When he created this deeply confrontational tragedy, Euripides ran the risk of incurring the disapproval of his entire audience. This may well explain why the judges placed him last in the competition in 431 BCE. But the clashes of values, the emotional tension, the masterly plot development and the radical *dénouement* which Euripides contrived in *Medea* have ensured its success both in later antiquity and from the Renaissance right through to the present day when it is the most often performed of all the surviving Greek tragedies.[12]

2 Medea

One modern writer summarizes the character of Medea as follows:

> In the figure of Medea, Euripides has created perhaps his most complex and ambiguous character: a figure who is in many ways attractive yet whose actions are the most repellent in tragedy; a barbarian

who espouses Greek ideals; a woman who draws on her femininity to do battle with men, yet whose ultimate vengeance involves the rejection of her most female instincts. There is no simple answer as to how we should regard Medea, for the justice of her cause is set in tension with the horror of her actions; the strength of her arguments with the manipulative and deceitful way she approaches other characters. The ending of the play is particularly troubling, for far from the crushed and distraught woman we might anticipate, we see an unrepentant and powerful Medea, leaving to pursue her murderous agenda elsewhere.[13]

This summary is a good starting point as we try to work out how to perform the title role. I agree that Medea is complex, almost certainly the most complex character in the surviving Greek tragedies, but I do not think that she is ambiguous. The contradictions which Swift lists are indeed innate in Medea's character as Euripides portrays it, but they refer to different roles, between which Medea moves as the play unfolds in performance. Euripides was not painting a static picture in which all the facets of a character can be viewed simultaneously but writing a dynamic play in which now one, now another aspect of Medea predominates. As I have argued in section 1, Medea develops from weak to strong to overwhelming, and while I have given reasons why she would have divided the judgements of both male and female members of the original audience, Swift's summary shows that she can be no less divisive today.

To direct and act this play properly, it is essential to differentiate between two modes in which Medea operates. On the one hand lies the deceptive Medea, determined to persuade and therefore performing a role in a relatively benign way with the Women of Corinth on her first entry (214ff.) and with Aegeus (Scene 4), and in a totally destructive way with Creon (271ff.) and with Jason on his second appearance (Scene 5). On the other lies the sincere Medea who is heard crying out behind the scenes before she enters for the first time, in Scene 1 and Choros 1; when she tells the Women her plans in 772ff.; in her asides when Jason is engaging with their sons (900ff., 922ff.); in the tortured monologue after the boys have returned from delivering the poisoned robe and crown (1021ff.); in her exit speech before murdering them (1242ff., quoted above); and in the Finale. These two aspects of Medea, performative and sincere, are bound together by the simple facts that in a patriarchal world, the only way for a woman to succeed against male opposition was to deceive and that it is natural for a woman to express grief first at being isolated, abandoned by her husband and then again – far more so – at having no choice, to achieve her revenge, except to kill her own children. To give coherence to this highly intelligent character and respond adequately to the part that Euripides has written for her, it is necessary for the actress to portray primarily the sane and rational Medea as performed by Diana Rigg but to include occasional elements of the half-demented woman, under the stress of almost intolerable provocation, presented by Fiona Shaw.[14] This is the approach which Claudia Bedford, under my direction, adopted in the premiere production of this translation.

3 Jason

The voyage of Argo was already 'much sung about' when Homer composed the *Odyssey* (12.70); the poet mentions that Jason was 'dear to' Hera, and indeed that goddess requested Aphrodite to imbue Medea with the passion for Jason which made his acquisition of the Golden Fleece possible. One wonders however if the lost early songs portrayed Jason as he appears in Apollonius of Rhodes' epic poem *The Voyage of Argo* (third century BCE, and so after Euripides); there he is frequently described as *amēchanos*, 'at a loss' – a very different adjective from Homer's characterizations of the heroes of the *Iliad* and *Odyssey*. Jason was probably already not among the greatest of legendary Greek heroes before Euripides' portrayal of him in his three appearances in *Medea*. In this play, he cuts a poor figure, both in terms of classical Athenian and of modern values, and is terribly punished for it – though, as one of the Women of Corinth remarks, justly so (1232).

First and foremost, he has broken the sacred oaths of fidelity to Medea that he swore by the gods in return for her enabling him to perform the otherwise impossible tasks set for him by Aietes and killing the serpent so they could escape with the Golden Fleece. Next, in marrying Creon's daughter, he is abandoning his duty as *kyrios* (the responsible adult male) to both Medea and his sons; his idea that their sons will be equal in Corinth with his future sons by the princess (563ff., 914ff.) is delusory, as they would be considered bastards and be under the eye of a jealous young stepmother. So the new marriage is, despite what he says at 547ff., beneficial only to him (he would swap refugee status for the position of heir to the throne of Corinth); it is of no value to Medea or to their children.

Jason's arguments are sophistic – and as such would have been viewed with suspicion by many in the Athenian audience; in particular, the idea (526ff.) that Aphrodite was responsible for his salvation in Colchis, not Medea whom the goddess had made to fall in love with him. Divine causation did not, in normal Greek thought of this period, take personal responsibility away from a human being. This is evident when someone tries to disclaim responsibility for his or her misdeeds on the ground of divine intervention, as does Helen in Euripides' later play *Women of Troy* (923ff; cf. Hecuba's rebuttal at 987ff.), but equally, it is pertinent when a human has performed a beneficial action under the influence of a god; only by sophistry can Jason deny (*almost* completely, see 532–3) that Medea herself saved his life and his mission. Then there is his eulogy of the benefits that Medea has received by coming to Greece (536ff.); in her present situation, condemned to exile, the reassurance that she now 'knows justice and the rule of law' is highly ironic consolation for what she has lost (cf. 481ff.). Finally, the blunt question, 'Why d'you need children?' (565) disregards the bond between mother and child (which, concededly, Medea will later violate in the most horrendous way to pursue her revenge to the bitter end). Jason would prefer women not to exist; his misogyny becomes apparent at 573–5.[15]

In their second scene together (Scene 5), Jason's lack of insight is apparent. He is totally deceived by Medea's feigned submission since the picture Medea paints of her 'repentant self' appeals to his ideal for women – that they should be 'sensible'. She is far too intelligent and subtle for Jason and even manages to explain away to his satisfaction the tears she sheds for the children, which the Women of Corinth and the audience know are caused by the fact that she is about to kill them (922–31).

The Finale raises a crucial issue; is the audience, ancient or modern, intended at the end of the play to feel some pity or sympathy for Jason, despite his gross shortcomings in the earlier scenes with Medea, now that he has lost his father-in-law, his bride and his sons? This is a question which can only be answered in performance; accordingly, it is considered in the 'Theatrical Commentary' later in this book, pp. 77ff.

4 Translation

George Steiner's massive essay on language and translation, *After Babel*,[16] demanded that good translation should attempt the impossible – a synthesis of literal fidelity to the source text and literate expression in the target language. Ancient Greek has a syntax and grammar which are very different from those of modern English, and the challenge of the Greek dramas to the contemporary translator is to be as accurate as possible (this is not the same as being literal), while also providing actable versions which enable a poetic drama to be played before audiences which have no live tradition of verse drama.[17] It is no service to Euripides' drama to present free or simplified adaptations, implying that the detailed content of the original tragedy is unimportant to the modern audience. This book is an attempt to rescue Euripides' original *Medea* both from loose textual adaptations and from overriding directorial 'concepts'.[18] But I am not at all opposed to entirely new plays based on the Medea story (or indeed any other Greek myth). Works such as Marina Carr's *By the Bog of Cats* operate in a different space – and one which the ancient playwrights would have approved because they themselves were not inhibited from presenting entirely different versions of the same story. (We can compare the three very different surviving versions of Orestes' return to avenge his father by committing matricide, Aeschylus' *Libation Bearers* and the *Electra* plays of Euripides and Sophocles.)

For this translation, as for my previous versions of Greek tragedy and comedy,[19] I attempted to find a language that would match the feel of the text as I experience it and to provide actors with 'hooks' – specific expressive words which they can use as a basis for creating physical gestures to illuminate the text. Only if this is done will they be able to generate a compelling modern English performance of Euripides' actual drama (as opposed to an adaptation or 'version') and to communicate its disturbingly topical content clearly to the audiences of today.[20] I wanted to present Euripides' meaning(s) as clearly and lucidly as possible, responding closely to the tone of each subsection and to the flow and shape of the drama as it unfolds. At times a decision had to be made between different interpretations of the original and whether specific lines were genuinely written by Euripides or were subsequent actors' or directors' interpolations.[21] But I was determined to avoid the infelicities and/or freedom from the original meaning which in my view mar some of the more recent published versions.[22]

The Greek poets tended to use different names for characters on different occasions, often to fit the metre. I have gone for consistency and recognizability, writing for example 'the Athenians' for 'the Sons of Erectheus' and 'The Sun' for Hēlios, and preferring Aphrodite to Cypris as the name of the goddess of love.

No attempt has been made to replicate in English the metrical forms (patterns of long and short syllables) and strophic response (see the following) of the original Greek; the source and target languages are too different from each other to justify such a procedure.[23] A sharp differentiation is however made between the five- to seven-beat line into which I have translated the spoken lines of the original Greek text and the much shorter lines, matching those of the original, in the anapaestic (chanted) and lyric (sung) sections. These sections are marked out in this translation by being double-indented.

There are almost no stage directions in our surviving texts of Greek drama – and none at all for *Medea*. I have added stage directions only where it is absolutely clear what must be happening and have reserved all conjectural moves for the 'Theatrical Commentary'.

Often translations of Greek tragedy take more English lines than those of the original Greek.[24] I have avoided this completely because it causes difficulty to students reading scholarship on the plays, which always refers to the standard line numbers of the Greek. And more importantly because it fails to match Euripides' concision, which is an important aspect of his art.

The lines spoken and sung by the choros are usually prefixed by the word 'Chorus' in translations. I have rejected this; the choros represented a collective character, a specific community of voices with which the solo characters interact. In this drama, they are Women of Corinth, and I have accordingly, as in my other translations, prefixed their lines not with what they *are* (a choros) but with the *character that they play*: Women of Corinth. And I use the Greek spelling 'choros' to remind readers and performers that the choros of Greek tragedy (and comedy) has a completely different role in the dramas from that of the chorus in an opera or musical.

The notations A1, A2, B1 and B2 beside the lyric stanzas of the choral odes denote groups of 'strophic' responding stanzas. The first pair of stanzas in an individual choral ode is lettered A and the second B; within each pair, the 1 stanza (*strophe*) was closely matched in metre by the 2 stanza (*antistrophe*), and the second stanza might perhaps have been choreographed to the same movements as the first or to movements representing a mirror image of those in the first. And while I have written 'Women' at the beginning of each of these odes, there is no good reason to suppose that the whole choros necessarily sung the whole of each song. Solo stanzas are conceivable for the ancient theatre and work well on the modern stage.[25] In our production, every choral utterance except the last line of the play was spoken by an individual. This enabled a contemporary production to engage with a modern audience in ways which are explored in the 'Theatrical Commentary', which follows the play text.

In this translation, all choral lines in dialogue scenes are assigned to '1 Woman', with the expectation that directors and actors will decide which member of the choros speaks each individual set of lines. The old idea that one individual was a 'Chorus Leader' and acted as a spokesperson for the rest of the choros has no ancient authority and results in a totally inadequate realization (and some frustrated actors) if insisted on in modern performance. Division is much more exciting, as it opens up many more possibilities for the movements of the choros. And why would the Athenian actors, performing for a mass audience which followed the plays with the same intensity as spectators at a modern football match, have avoided excitement?[26]

All translation involves some loss, and no wise translator could pretend to render all of Euripides' richness into English, but at least we can choose, carefully, what to keep in order to provide a version that is, to repeat my fundamental criteria (which are in creative tension with each other), both accurate and actable. I have tested this translation for actability in a professional production, making changes where my draft wording did not work in rehearsal.

There are no footnotes; no one can act a footnote, so the translation must be comprehensible in itself. The backstory and aftermath printed before and after the text are designed to provide the information necessary to understand the play, and there is a glossary of names at the end of the book for those unfamiliar with the mythical material that Euripides draws upon.

This translation is designed for actors; the punctuation is for them, not for readers. A comma indicates that a quick breath can be taken; semicolons and full stops allow for a longer pause – but not too long, as that disrupts the flow of the verse. Strong breaks during speeches are marked by a gap between lines.

5 The original conditions of performance

Greek tragedies were normally performed by up to three masked actors, changing masks and costumes to play different roles (though in *Medea*, the lead actor plays the role of Medea throughout), together with a choros which in Euripides' time numbered 15. The masks (the Greek word for them is *prosōpon*, meaning 'face') were realistic, covered the entire head and were essential to indicate to distant spectators the gender, age and status of each character. The location was the Theatre of Dionysus at Athens; see Figure 1.1 for its appearance in the fifth century. The playing area, the square or rectangular flat *orchēstra*, was surrounded on three sides by an audience of 6–10,000 in the *theatron*, rows of seats rising up the slopes

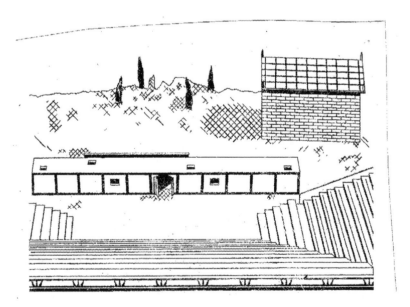

Figure 1.1 The Theatre of Dionysus in the mid fifth century BCE.
Source: M. Ewans

behind the theatre which led to the Acropolis. The performance space was backed by the *skēnē* building, which was a long narrow construction with one pair of doors and one or two windows; inside it, the actors changed masks and costumes to play different roles as the drama unfolded. In this play, it represents the house formerly occupied by Jason and Medea, and now by Medea alone with her sons and her slaves.

Not shown in the figure, because the nature of its construction is unknown, is the *mēchanē*, a crane based behind the *skēnē* on which characters, usually gods, could be flown in to hover above the *orchēstra* and address other characters in the playing space below. The appearance of Medea on the *mēchanē* at the end of this play is the first extant example of its use. There was no raised stage behind the *orchēstra*; solo characters entered directly into the *orchēstra* and shared it with the choros members when they were present, which was for most of the play.[27] Actors entered the *orchēstra* either through the double doors of the *skēnē* or through one of the two outdoors side entrances beside the front sectors of the audience (*eisodoi*). By a convention which originated in the actual location of the theatre, the stage left *eisodos* led to the downtown of the place in which the action is set, and the stage right *eisodos* led to the country and/or the port.[28] It is very noticeable that in *Medea* only one character, Aegeus, enters from and exits to the right *eisodos*. He is the only character who comes from, and goes to, another city; everyone else comes from and goes to downtown Corinth.

The Theatre of Dionysus was a simple and highly effective playing space, but its unwritten rules are very different from those of the modern proscenium arch stage. To give a key example, power is concentrated in the rear half of the *orchēstra*, advancing from the *skēnē* doors via back centre towards the centre point increases the power of a character, but as that character advances further than the centre into the front half of the *orchēstra*, he or she loses power as less and less of the audience can see and relate to their mask. By contrast in a proscenium arch theatre, an actor is in a more powerful position the nearer he or she is to the front row of the audience. And in the Theatre of Dionysus, actors needed to turn their backs on parts of the audience and could do this since the *skēnē* acted as a sounding board and reflected the voice back to the whole audience. (Those Greek theatres which survive relatively undamaged have excellent acoustics.)[29] It must be remembered that the masked male actors were viewed by spectators up to 100 metres away, so gestures would have had to be large to make any effect, and the relative position of actors in the *orchēstra* (blocking) was the main means by which the meaning of the text could be conveyed in action.

For this reason, our research was centred on a production in a proscenium arch theatre to elucidate the difficulties which are created when adapting for an end-on audience in an intimate indoor theatre a drama designed for a large audience surrounding the playing space on three sides in the open air.[30] The results are embodied in the 'Theatrical Commentary', which follows the play text in this book.

6 *Medea* today

This play has deep resonance for contemporary audiences. It raises many issues that are important today, including the place of immigrants in society and above all the power relationships between the genders. Medea's polemic speech on the lot of women (230ff.) was neglected for over 2,000 years; its sentiments were not echoed until the Enlightenment of the eighteenth century and then only relatively feebly. It is therefore not surprising that the suffragettes declaimed it during their campaigns in the late nineteenth and early twentieth centuries. Nor have her points been wholly answered by the reforms of the twentieth and twenty-first centuries; coercive control and domestic violence against women are all too common today, even if in most western societies divorce is now easier for women trapped in an intolerable marriage.

Filicide is an extreme act, but it was not invented by Euripides, even though he was the first to portray Medea killing her children. Ino (cited by the Women at 1283ff.) was not the only example in Greek myth (Procne immediately comes to mind), and Aristophanes' Lysistrata states bluntly that:

> No wonder the tragedies are all about us;
> We just fuck and get rid of the babies.
>
> (139–40)

So filicide happened in ancient Greek society. It is also present in modern western society; up to 50% of all children who are murdered are killed by one of their parents.[31] Their only difference from Medea is that, not having the chariot of the Sun to escape in, the criminal parent often commits suicide after the murder or murders.

This contemporary resonance makes the play deeply disturbing to a modern audience (and indeed to the cast and crew). Accordingly, strategies have to be devised to convey on stage its full horror and compelling tragic force. We aimed in our production for intensity and flow so that Euripides' remarkable tragedy could unfold unremittingly.

Notes

1 It is unlikely that Neophron's *Medea*, in which Medea also kills her own children, was created before Euripides': Page argued this in 1938 (xxxii–xxxvi). Cf. e.g. McDermott 1989: 9–24; Mossman 2011: 23–9; *pace* e.g. Thompson 1944;

Michelini 1989. Johnston (1997: 65–6) claimed without providing evidence that the myth that Medea killed her own children (rather than the Corinthians in retaliation for the deaths of their king and princess) predates Euripides, but even if this were so, he was almost certainly the first playwright to *dramatize* this version of the legend.

2 Medea's affinity to Homeric and Sophoclean heroes was argued in an influential article by Knox (first published in 1977; best known in the 1979 reprint). Cf. also Bongie 1977.

3 This was established by Adkins (1960: 226–32), citing among other texts Meno's definition of *aretē* in Plato's eponymous dialogue (71e2ff.).

4 Reeve 1972; Diggle 1984.

5 See 'Translation Notes', pp. 58–9.

6 I cannot agree with Mossman (2011: 317–18, 329–32), who argues for deletion of 1078–80. See 'Translation Notes', p. 59.

7 Page 1938: xiv.

8 Cf. Knox 1979: 306–7.

9 Especially in opera; cf. Ewans 2007: 60–9.

10 In myth cf. Ino (cited by the Women at 1283ff.) and Procne, and for daily life cf. Aristophanes *Lysistrata* 139–40, cited on p. 14.

11 The issue of whether women attended the performances of drama at the festival has been much debated. I believe it is settled by Aristophanes *Peace* 960ff., a joke which is simply incomprehensible if women were not sitting at the back of the theatre. Cf. Olson 1988: 254–5 *ad loc.*, with references.

12 The best scholarly treatment of *Medea* is Swift 2016. On the reception of *Medea* cf. Hall, Mcintosh and Taplin (eds.) 2001. For a record of modern performances, visit the website of the Archive of Performances of Greek and Roman Drama.

13 Swift 2016: 18.

14 See Hall 2010: 19. It is very unfortunate that neither of these classic performances was preserved on video.

15 He does not rave on about the evils of women, as Hippolytus does in Euripides' next surviving drama (*Hippolytus* 616–68), but both men come to a bad end because of their rejection of a woman.

16 Steiner 1975: Chapter 4 *passim*.

17 *Medea* has been translated into prose by Moorwood 2008; Studdart 2014. This is totally unacceptable for performance (and should be for study as well); a prose version is, however, legitimate when it is done by an editor to elucidate her vision of the literal meaning of the Greek text, as in Mossman 2011.

18 Ben Power's 2014 'version' for the National Theatre of Great Britain was so inaccurate that it can only be regarded as a grossly free adaptation.

19 Ewans 1995, 1996, 1999, 2000, 2010, 2011.

20 Kenneth McLeish and Frederic Raphael's translation, used by Deborah Warner in her famous 2000 production starring Fiona Shaw, comes close.

21 Two modern commentaries on the Greek text have been very helpful: Mastronade 2002; (especially) Mossman 2011. For the solutions to disputed passages which are adopted in this version, see 'Translation Notes', pp. 57–9.

22 E.g. Svarlien 2008 (freedom); Taplin 2013 (infelicities). Blondell 1999 is much more accurate, but the verse is often jerky and lacks flow. Rayor 2013 is fairly accurate and has (unlike previous translations) been workshopped and performed, but to my ears, it too lacks flow, and although the text is lineated as verse, it is hard to detect a rhythm. Additionally, she would have benefited from consulting Mossman's 2011 edition of the Greek text.

23 This has been attempted on occasion, but it forces the translator to go too far away from the meaning of the Greek. In any case, English verse does not normally consist of patterns of long and short syllables, as Greek verse did, so the effort is largely wasted.

24 E.g. Svarlien 2008, and most of the translations in the Oxford University Press New York series.

25 For subdivision of choral lyrics and anapaests between individuals in classical Greek productions, cf. Ewans 1995: xxiv–xxv + notes.

26 On the audiences' emotional responses to tragic performance, cf. Stanford 1983. Against the idea of a spokesperson, cf. Ewans 1995: xxiii–xxiv. For a good example of a scene that benefits enormously from division of the dialogue between different members of the choros, cf. Aeschylus *Eumenides* scene 2, where Apollo tries to drive the Furies out of his temple, and they interrogate him. Cf. Ewans (forthcoming).

27 Cf. Ley and Ewans 1985; Ewans 1995: xx–xxii, with bibliography; also Wiles 1997: 63–86; Ley 2006: ix ff.; Ewans 2011: 215.

28 Rehm 1992: 154.

29 E.g. Epidaurus and Delphi. The *theatron* of the Theatre of Dionysus itself has suffered major damage, and the ruins of a Roman-era theatre with a semicircular *orchēstra* and a raised stage conceal the original fifth-century playing space.

30 Despite the flurry of interest in stagecraft by classical scholars since the publication of Taplin 1977, no one to my knowledge has addressed this issue properly (Goldhill 2007: 7–44 touches on it, but he had not directed any Greek plays himself). The question of adaptation to the available performance space is, however, fundamental to modern production since only a few contemporary theatres have an audience surrounding the action on three sides and can therefore perform Greek dramas as they were originally intended to be seen.

31 On infanticide in modern society and its relevance to *Medea*, cf. Easterling 1977; Hall 2010; Mossman 2011: 1–2.

EURIPIDES
Medea

DOI: 10.4324/9781003215844-2

The backstory

Pelias usurped the throne legitimately held by his stepbrother Aison in Iolcus in Thessaly; Jason was Aison's son, and his mother, suspecting Pelias might kill Jason to prevent him from claiming the throne, had him brought up elsewhere. When Jason, now a grown man, returned to Iolcus, Pelias recognized him and persuaded him to attempt to recover the Golden Fleece in the possession of Aietes, king of Colchis (on the east coast of the Black Sea). He hoped that Jason would not return alive.

Jason gathered a band of heroes who set sail on the ship Argo, and after many adventures they arrived in Colchis. Aietes was unwilling to part with the Fleece and challenged one of the Argonauts to plough a large field with two fire-breathing bulls, sow it with dragon's teeth and then fight the armed men who would spring up as a crop.

Medea, who had magical powers, was Aietes' teenage daughter. She fell in love with Jason, and with the aid of her spells he was able to tame the bulls unscathed and got the armed men to fight each other. Medea also magically killed the sleepless serpent which was guarding the Fleece so Jason could retrieve it. Aietes was suspicious, but Medea warned the Argonauts to escape and killed her brother Apsyrtus, so Aietes was delayed in his pursuit; the Argonauts escaped with the Fleece – and Medea. After further adventures, they returned to Iolcus, where Medea took revenge for Jason on Pelias, who was now quite old. She successfully rejuvenated an aged ram by cooking it in a cauldron with magic herbs; she then persuaded Pelias' daughters to repeat the experiment on their father but did not give them the right herbs, and Pelias died.

Jason and Medea fled to Corinth, where for some years they lived in harmony and had two sons. But then Jason made a disastrous decision, and that's when the play begins.

Characters in order of appearance

NURSE
TUTOR
TWO SONS
WOMEN OF CORINTH
MEDEA
CREON, KING OF CORINTH
JASON
AEGEUS, KING OF ATHENS
MESSENGER

Silent roles

ATTENDANT ON MEDEA (FEMALE)
(CREON'S SOLDIERS)
(AEGEUS' ATTENDANTS)

*

Text which is double-indented was chanted or sung in the original performance.

The indications (A1), (A2), (B1) (B2) in the choral odes indicate stanzas which were in metrical correspondence to each other in the original Greek (*strophe* and *antistrophe*).

Set: the façade of a house, with one set of double doors at the centre and a window. There are also side entrances further downstage on both the left and the right.

MEDEA

Scene 1

Enter NURSE from the house

NURSE   If only the ship Argo'd never flown
to Colchis through the dark-blue Clashing Rocks;
If only in the glades of Pēlion
the pine was never felled to make the oars
for the heroic men who went to fetch   5
the Golden Fleece for Pelias. Medea then,
my mistress, never would have sailed
to Iolcus' towers, stricken by love for Jason.
She wouldn't have persuaded the daughters of Pelias
to kill their father, and have settled here in Corinth   10
with her husband and her children, giving pleasure in her exile
to the citizens where she has come to live,
and always in agreement with Jason.
That is the best security,
when the wife does not quarrel with her husband.   15

But as things are all's enmity; the closest bonds are now diseased.
Jason's betrayed his children and my mistress, since
he's sleeping in a royal marriage-bed;
he's married to the daughter of Creon, the ruler of this land.

Wretched Medea's had her honour stripped away;   20
she cries 'Our oaths!' and calls upon
the great pledge of their right hands, summoning the gods
to witness just how shabby a return Jason has given her.
She's lying down, refusing food, submitting to her suffering,
wasting away, dissolved in tears,   25
because she knows her husband's treated her unjustly.
She will not raise her eyes or lift her face
from staring at the floor; and when her friends
give her advice, she listens like a rock or wave.
But sometimes, turning her white neck away,   30
she grieves alone for her dear father,
for her homeland and palace – all that she betrayed
to come here with the man who's now dishonoured her.
Disaster's taught this miserable woman just
how great a thing it is not to desert your native land.   35
She hates her children, takes no joy in seeing them.
I fear she may be planning something new,   37
for she is terrible; if someone makes an enemy of her   44
he will not easily sing out a song of victory.   45

Enter TUTOR and SONS, left.

Here come her sons; they've been out for a run.
They know nothing about their mother's agony –
a young mind does not often suffer pain.
TUTOR   You've long been one of my mistress' slaves;
why are you standing here outside the doors,   50
lamenting your misfortunes to yourself?
Why does Medea want you to leave her alone?
NURSE   Agèd attendant on the sons of Jason,
when their masters' fortunes suffer a bad turn,
that seizes on the heart of good slaves too.   55
I've come to such a pitch of anguish that
I felt a longing to come here and tell
to earth and heaven all my mistress' hard luck.
TUTOR   Has the poor woman not yet stopped grieving?
NURSE   I envy you your ignorance; her suffering has just begun.   60
TUTOR   O foolish woman! – if I dare to call my mistress that –
for she knows nothing of her latest misery.
NURSE   What is it, old man? Don't grudge me the truth.
TUTOR   It's nothing. I regret what I just said.

NURSE   Please don't conceal this from your fellow-slave.   65
     I will keep silence, if I must.
TUTOR   I went where they play draughts, where older men
     gather around the spring of Peirēnē; and there I heard
     – without seeming to overhear – a man say that the king,
     Creon, is going to throw these boys out   70
     together with their mother from this land.
     I don't know if this story's true; I hope it's not.
NURSE   Will Jason let his children suffer this,
     even if he has a quarrel with their mother?   75
TUTOR   Old marriage-bonds are now supplanted by new ones,
     and he is not a friend to this household.
NURSE   Then we are lost, if we must add this new evil
     before we've drained the old one to the dregs.
TUTOR   It's not the time for our mistress to learn this news;   80
     so you must hol your peace and not tell her.
NURSE   Children, do you hear how your father's treating you?
     I do not wish him dead, for he's my master; but he has
     been caught out doing wrong to his own family.
TUTOR   What human being doesn't? Have you just recognized   85
     that everybody loves himself more than his
     fellow men, since in pursuit of sex their father loves   86
     these kids no more?   88
NURSE   Children, go inside the house; all will be well.
     Tutor, you must take special care to keep them on their own   90
     and do not let them near their mother in her present mood.
     I have already seen her turn a glance as fearsome as a bull's
     upon them, as if she intends to act; for I am sure
     she will not cease her anger till it strikes someone.
     I only hope she harms her enemies, not friends.   95

MEDEA   *(inside the house)*
     Ah!
     Unfortunate and wretched in my troubles,
     Oh! Oh! I wish I could die!
NURSE   This is it, dear children; your mother's
     stirring up her heart and stirring up her rage.
     Get indoors quickly, and don't go   100
     where she can see you –
     don't approach her; guard against
     the savage character and hate-filled nature
     of her stubborn mind.
     Go now, go in quick as you can.   105

Exeunt TUTOR and BOYS into the house.

It's clear; a thundercloud of lamentation's
rising up – and she'll set it aflame
with greater passion; what will her mighty
soul without restraint do now,
bitten by calamities?   110

MEDEA   *Aiai!*
I'm miserable, I've suffered, suffered harm
that deserves to be cried aloud. Curst children
of a hateful mother, perish with your father –
let the whole house be destroyed.

NURSE   Oh, I pity you.   115
How do the boys share in their father's crime?
Why do you hate them? Oh children,
I am terribly afraid that you will suffer.
The temperaments of royalty are fearsome;
because they're almost unrestrained   120
and are so powerful, it is rare
for them to overcome their rage.

To be accustomed to live in equality
is best; at least may it be granted me
to lead a moderate life, and grow securely to old age.
Just to speak of moderation wins   125
first prize, and to practice it is far
the best for mortal men.
Excess does not yield any gain,
for when a god is angry with a house
it pays with great destruction.   130

Choros 1

Enter WOMEN OF CORINTH, left.

WOMEN   I heard the voice, I heard the cry
of the unhappy one from Colchis.
Is she not yet calm? Tell us, old woman.
I heard her outburst from inside   135
the house, and I do not rejoice
at suffering in this home,
since I am bound to it by friendship.

NURSE	This home does not exist; that has already gone.	
	The husband's sleeping with a princess, while	140
	my mistress wastes away her life-force	
	in her room, not comforted in any way	
	by words from those who hold her dear.	
MEDEA	*Aiai!*	
	I wish a lightning bolt would strike my head!	
	What gain is it for me to stay alive?	145
	Oh! Oh! In death I'd be at rest,	
	leaving this hateful life.	
WOMEN	(A1) Zeus, Earth and Light,	
	D' you hear the cry which this	
	miserable wife sings?	150
	You fool, what is this love for death's horrendous bed?	
	Will you hasten on your end?	
	Don't pray for this.	
	If your husband now worships a new girl,	155
	do not let this sharpen up your anger;	
	Zeus will help you to seek justice.	
	Don't waste away in mourning for your bedmate.	
MEDEA	Themis the great and powerful Artemis,	160
	do you see what I suffer, I who bound	
	my cursèd husband with great oaths?	
	I wish I could see both him and his bride	
	destroyed together with their house	
	because they dare to do me such injustice,	
	unprovoked.	165
	Oh my father, oh my city, from which I departed	
	shamefully, killing my own brother.	
NURSE	Do you hear what she says, and how her cries invoke	
	by special prayer Themis and Zeus, who is the guardian	
	of oaths for human beings?	170
	There's no way that my mistress will do something small	
	to bring her anger to an end.	
WOMEN	(A2) I wish she could come out into our sight	
	and hear us speak,	175
	to see if somehow she might find release	
	from her deep anger and the passion of her mind.	
	Never let my strong goodwill	
	for this friend go away.	
	Go, and get her to come out;	180
	say that we're on her side.	

Hurry, before she does some harm
to those inside; her grief is rushing headlong.

NURSE   I'll do that; but I fear
I won't persuade my mistress.   185
Still, I'll do this favour to you – though it's difficult.
She glowers like a bull, a lioness
protecting cubs, whenever one of us
comes near to speak to her.

You would not be wrong if you called   190
those men of old stupid and fools,
who composed pleasant sounds
for feasts and banquets and for dinner parties:
no one's found ways to stop men's   195
hateful sufferings with music and with sounds
of many strings – sufferings which lead to death,
and terrible misfortunes which destroy a house.
It would be great if we could soothe our ills with melodies;
but why do they sing loud songs for so long in vain
just so that banquets may be satisfying?   200
The fullness of the feast gives people
pleasure in itself.

Exit NURSE into the house.

WOMEN   I heard the mournful cry of her laments;   205
she shouts out grievously against
the wicked husband who's betrayed her bed.
Suffering injustice, she calls on the gods –
Zeus' consort Themis, guardian of oaths,
who made her travel past the straits to Greece   210
passing by night across the salty barrier
of the Black Sea that few can cross.

Scene 2

Enter MEDEA from the house.

MEDEA   Women of Corinth, I have come outside
so you may not blame me. For I know many men   215
have turned out to be haughty, some away from public view,
others outside their doors; then there are those who by

behaving quietly become accused of laziness.
For there's no justice in the eyes of men
who hate someone on sight, before they've clearly learnt   220
his character, and when they have not suffered an injustice.
A foreigner must specially be pleasing to the city;
but I can't praise a citizen who is so stubborn that
he's bitter to his fellow-citizens because of his sheer ignorance.

This unexpected burden that's fallen on me   225
has wrecked my soul; I am as good as dead,
I've lost the love of life and want to die, my friends.
I know well – I put all my trust in one,
my husband, who's turned out to be the worst of men.

Of every creature that's alive and capable of thought   230
we women are most wretched.
First we must buy a husband with a massive dowry,
then subject our bodies to his mastery –
and that's the worse of the two evils.
In this the stakes are very high – whether we get   235
a bad man or a good one, since divorce is difficult
for women, and we can't refuse a husband's right to sex.
A woman has to be a prophetess – she's come into new habits
and new customs, and she hasn't learnt at home
how best to cope with her new bedmate.   240
Then suppose we work everything out well,
and our husband enjoys his being yoked to us,
our life is blessed; if it's not, we ought to die.
If what is happening at home vexes a husband,
he can go out and find relief from stress –   245
but we are forced to be dependent on one man.   247
Men say we live a safe life in the home,
while they do battle with the spear.
But they are wrong; I'd rather stand three times   250
with shield in hand than give birth once.

But you and I are differently placed;
you have a city of your own, your fathers' homes,
enjoyment of your life, the company of friends –
while I'm alone, without a city, and I'm being treated
                                                  shamefully   255
by my own husband, who abducted me from far away.
I have no mother, brother, or another relative with whom

I could find a safe haven after this catastrophe.
I want to ask you just one thing;
if I can find some means or some device   260
to pay my husband justly for these wrongs,   261
be silent. In other things a woman's full of fear,   263
cowardly when it comes to battle and confronting swords;
but when she finds she has been wronged in bed,   265
there is no other heart that has more thirst for blood.

1 WOMAN   I will do that; it's just for you to punish your husband,
Medea. I don't wonder that you grieve your fate.
But now I see the ruler of this land, Creon;
he's coming, and will tell you his new plans.   270

Enter CREON left, with SOLDIERS.

CREON   You, the sullen one who's angry with her husband,
Medea, I proclaim that you must leave this land an exile,
taking your two children with you;
and do not delay. I am here to enforce this,
and I will not go home   275
before I cast you out beyond the frontiers of this land.
MEDEA   *Aiai!* I'm desperate, I'm utterly destroyed;
my enemies proceed full-sail, and there's no easy way
for me to disembark from this disaster.
Yet, despite my sufferings, I will still ask: 280
why are you sending me away from here, Creon?
CREON   I am afraid – there is no need to conceal what I mean –
that you will do irreparable harm to my daughter.
I've several reasons for this fear;
you're clever, you know many means of harm,   285
and you are bitter that your man no longer sleeps with you.
I've also heard – people have told me – that you've threatened
to do something to the father of the bride, to her
and to her husband. I will prevent that happening.
It's better to incur your anger now, woman,   290
than to be softened and lament it later on.
MEDEA   No! No!
Creon, it's not just now but often that
my reputation's wounded me and done great harm.
A man who has his wits about him never should
bring up his children to be very clever;   295

apart from criticisms of their idleness,
they incur jealous enmity from other citizens.
Bringing new subtleties to lesser minds
you'll seem to be inept and quite unwise;
and if you are considered better in the city than those who   300
know complex things, you will be put down as a troublemaker.
I myself suffer this fate;
I'm clever, and this makes some people jealous.   303
Others find me irksome; but I'm not *that* clever.   305
You are afraid of me, that you will suffer some misfortune?
That is not how I am, so do not fear, Creon,
that I would harm the royal house.
How have *you* wronged me? You've betrothed your daughter
to the man you want. I hate my husband;   310
you, I think, made the marriage with a level head.
So now I feel no jealousy if you do well;
have your marriage, prosper – but please let me live
here in this land. I have been wronged, but I
will keep the peace; I have been conquered by a higher power.   315

CREON   You say words which are gentle; but I fear
that in your heart you're planning something bad.
I trust you even less than I have done before,
A woman of sharp temper – or indeed a man –
is easier to guard against than one who's clever and
                                             stays silent.   320
Leave quick as you can, say nothing more,
for this is fixed, and you have no skill which
will let you stay here, since you are my enemy.

MEDEA   *(approaching CREON)*
Don't do this, by your knees and the new bride.

CREON   You're wasting words; you never will persuade me.   325

MEDEA   Will you exile me, pay no reverence to my prayer?

CREON   Yes; I do not care for you more than my family.

MEDEA   Oh native land, how much I think of you.

CREON   Besides my children, it's the dearest thing to me as well.

MEDEA   Oh, how great an evil love is to mankind.   330

CREON   No, I am sure that depends on circumstances.

MEDEA   Zeus, don't forget the man who started all this evil.

CREON   Go, foolish creature; free me from my troubles.

MEDEA   You have troubles; I have many more.

CREON   Swiftly my men will push you out.   335

MEDEA   *(falls at Creon's feet and takes his hand in both of hers)*
          Don't do that, I beg you, Creon.
CREON   It seems you'll be a nuisance, woman.
MEDEA   I'll go into exile; that's not what I'm begging you.
CREON   Then why are you still pressing me, holding my hand?
MEDEA   Just let me stay for this one day   340
          and think about my plans for exile,
          and some resources for my sons, since their father
          does not care enough to secure aid for them.
          Please pity them; you are a father too, so it is natural
          for you to have good will to them.   345
          I am not thinking of myself, if we must go,
          but I lament for them, made needy by misfortune.
CREON   My nature is not really tyrannical,
          and by showing respect I've often caused calamity.
          Now I can see that I am doing wrong, woman;   350
          but still you'll get your wish. I tell you this;
          if dawn tomorrow sees you and your sons
          still in my territory,
          you will die; this is a true word.
          But now, if you must stay, stay this one day;   355
          you won't do any of the ghastly things I fear.

Exeunt CREON and SOLDIERS, left.

WOMEN   Your sufferings have made you miserable,   358
          unhappy woman;   357
          where will you turn? What friend,
          what house, what land will save you from your troubles?   360
          The gods have thrown you, Medea,   362
          into a surge of troubles that can't be escaped.
MEDEA   It's bad in every way, that cannot be denied.
          But things won't stay like this – do not think that.   365
          The newlyweds will still face challenges,
          and there will be great suffering for Creon.
          D'you think I ever would have fawned on him
          if not for my advantage, something that I can devise?
          I never would have spoken to him, or have touched him
                                                    with my hands.   370
          Now he has been so foolish that
          when he was capable of wrecking all my plans
          by throwing me out of this land, he gave me this one day

to stay, in which I'll kill three of my enemies –
the father and the bride and my husband.   375
I've many ways to make them die,
but friends, I do not know which to try first.
Shall I consume the bridal home with fire,
or thrust a sharpened sword into their guts,
creeping silently inside the house and to their marriage-bed?   380
But there's one thing against that; if I'm caught
going into the house and then attempting this,
I'll die, and be a laughingstock for all my enemies.
Best is the most straightforward way, in which we have
the greatest skill – to strike them dead with poison drugs.   385

Well:
suppose they're dead. What city will receive me?
What friend will let me live where I cannot be seized,
and have a secure home, so that my body will be safe?
It cannot be. I'll wait a little while,
and if a safe refuge appears for me   390
I will pursue this murder with deceit and silence.
But if something that I can't handle drives me out
I'll take a sword myself, and even if I'm going to die
I'll kill them, going to the violent heights of daring.
I swear by Hekatē, the goddess whom I worship   395
most of all, and choose for my companion in this plan,   396
that none of them will rejoice and injure my heart.   398
(Her shrine is a hearth deep inside my house.)   397
I'll make their wedding bitter, full of grief,
bitter their union and my exile from this land.   400

So come now, don't spare any of the things you know,
Medea; you have planned it and devised it –
do the deed of terror; now the contest is for you to show your
                                                              courage.
Do you see what you suffer? You cannot be made a laughingstock
by Jason's marriage to a descendant of Sisyphus   405
when you're the daughter of a noble man, granddaughter
                                              of a god, the Sun.
And you know how to do it; also we were born
as women, very helpless when it comes to doing good,
but very wise creators of all kinds of harm.

Exit MEDEA into the house.

Choros 2

WOMEN (A1) The streams of sacred rivers run uphill,   410
and justice and all else is turned around:
it's men who plan deceitful tricks, and there's
no trust in oaths sworn by the gods.
What people say will turn my life around to
good repute;   415
honour is coming to the female sex;
we won't be tarnished by malicious talk.   420

(A2) The muses of the old poets will cease singing their songs
immortalizing our unfaithfulness;
Apollo, lord of melodies,
did not give us the inspired sounds   425
Of lyres, since I would then have sung new songs
opposing men. The long expanse of time has much to tell
about females as well as males.   430

(B1) You sailed out from your father's house
with your heart crazed by love; you travelled through
the Bosporus, and came to live in a strange land   435
where, desperate woman, you have lost the husband
from your bed,
and they are driving you dishonoured into exile.

(B2) The lovely grace of oaths has gone, and there is no respect
for them left in the whole of Greece; shame's flown up
to the heavens.   440
Unhappy one, you cannot go back to your father's home
for a new anchorage, free from your sufferings;
a princess stronger than your marriage-bed
stands in authority over your house.   445

Scene 3

Enter JASON, left; enter MEDEA from the house.

JASON   I've seen not now but many times
that a sharp temper is an evil that can't be controlled.
You could have lived in a house in this land

bearing without demur the plans of your superiors,
but thanks to foolish words you have become an exile.   450
It's no big deal for me; just keep on saying
Jason is the very worst of men.
But as for what you've said against the royal family
consider it a blessing that exile's your only punishment.
As for me, I always tried to moderate   455
the anger of the king, and wanted you to stay;
but you persisted in your folly, always badmouthing
the ruler; that is why you're banished from this land.
Despite all this I've come, I have not given up
on my loved ones; I'm looking out for you, lady,   460
so you won't leave here with the children destitute
or needing anything. Exile brings many troubles.
Even if you hate me,
I could not ever think badly of you.

MEDEA   You're utterly despicable! This is the   465
worst rebuke that I can give to your unmanliness.
You've come to me, you've come although you are
most hated by me and the gods and the whole human race.
It is not courage or an act of bravery
to confront friends whom you have treated wrongly;   470
it's the greatest of diseases known to man –
shamelessness. But you have done well to come;
by speaking out against your evil I will be lightened
inside my soul, and you will feel pain as you hear.

I will go back to the beginning;   475
I saved you, as all of the Greeks know well
who sailed with you upon the ship Argo,
when you were sent to master the fire-breathing bulls with yokes,
and sow the deadly crop;
and then I killed the snake who held the Golden Fleece   480
tight in his many coils and never slept;
I brought to you the light of salvation.
I then chose to betray my father and my home
to come to Pēlian Iolcus with you –
eager, and most unwise;   485
and I killed Pelias, in the worst kind of death
at his own daughters' hands, and wrecked the entire house.

After I'd done this for you, worst of men,
you have betrayed me, and got a new wife
when we have children; for if you were still childless   490
it would have been forgivable for you to yearn
               for this new marriage-bed.
All trust in oaths is gone, and I don't know
if you think that the gods no longer rule
or that there are new laws for men,
since you know well that you have broken oaths to me.   495
Oh, my right hand, which you so often took in yours
and knees of mine, in vain you have been supplicated by
an evil man, and we have lost our hopes.
Come, I will share something with you as a relative
(I don't expect anything good from you – but I will try,   500
since when you're asked you will appear shameful).
Where can I turn? Back to my father's house,
which I betrayed – also my country – to come here with you?
Or to the wretched daughters of Pelias? Yes, I'm very sure
they'd gladly welcome me, their father's murderer.   505

The situation's this; I have become an enemy
to my loved ones at home, and there are people I should
               not have wronged,
whom I have made hostile to do favours to you.
Oh yes, you made me blessed in the eyes of many Greek
women in recompense; but I am now wretched –
with a marvellous and faithful husband!—   510
If I will have to flee expelled from here
bereft of friends, alone with children who will also be alone.
What a fine reproach for you, the new bridegroom,
that your boys wander, beggars, and the woman who
               saved you.   515
Oh Zeus, why have you given us clear signs to tell
if gold has been adulterated,
but there's no sign upon the body of a man
by which we can find out who's evil?

1 WOMAN Anger is terrible and hard to cure   520
    when relatives are locked in mutual strife.
JASON   It seems I must show that I'm good at speaking,
    but like a skilful captain of a ship
    reef my sails tightly, so as to escape
    your uncontrolled outpouring, woman.   525

I for my part, since you build too much upon my debt to you,
declare that only the goddess of love
– no other god or human being – saved my voyage.
You have a subtle mind; but it would be invidious to tell
how Eros with his arrows that can't be escaped   530
compelled you to save me.
I will not give quite all of the credit to him,
for when you helped me things went well.
But you gained more from saving me
than what you gave; and I will tell you how.   535
First, you now live in Greece instead of a barbarian land
and you know justice and the rule of law
which ensures violence does not have free rein.
And all Greeks know of you and your reputation
for cleverness; if you still lived on the furthest boundaries   540
of Earth, no one would have known of you.
May I have neither gold stored in my house
nor the ability to sing a sweeter song than Orpheus,
if I were not conspicuous for fame.

I've said all this about my own labours;   545
for you created this contest of words.
As for your objections to my royal marriage,
in this I'll show you first that I was wise
and prudent, then a great friend both to you
and to our children. *(MEDEA starts angrily)* No, be still.   550
When I came here from Iolcus,
bringing many problems that were hard to solve,
what better plan could I, an exile,
find than marrying the daughter of a king?
You're all worked up because you think I hated being
                         wed to you, 555
and was struck with desire for this new bride; but that is wrong.
Nor was I eager for a contest to create new children;
the ones I have are quite enough, and I'm content with them.
My reason was the most important, that we should live well
and not in need of anything, because I know   560
that everyone deserts a former friend when he is poor;
I could raise children in a way that's worthy of my house,
and when I father brothers to your sons
I might make them all equal, and by bringing them together
I would lead a happy life. Why d'you need children?   565

It is worthwhile to me for my two living sons
to profit by the future ones. Surely these plans are good?
And you would say so, if you were not worked up about sex.
It's got to such a point that when your sex life's fine
you women think that everything's all right;   570
but if some problem comes up about sex,
you look upon the best and fairest things
with complete enmity. I wish men could have children
in some other way, and there were no females.
Then there would be no evil.   575

1 WOMAN   Jason, you have embellished your speech well;
but, even if I speak against what you believe,
I think that in betraying your wife you have not been just.

MEDEA   In many ways I disagree with others.
I think the unjust man who can speak cleverly   580
incurs the greatest penalty;
for, feeling confident to cloak injustice in fair speech,
he dares the utmost villainy; but he is not clever enough.
Take you; don't put on a façade to me
and speak so cunningly; one word will knock you to
                                           the floor.   585
If you were not a wicked man, you should have made
this marriage *after* you'd persuaded me, not kept it secret.

JASON   Yes, I'm sure you would have given me support
if I'd told you about it – since not even now
will you abandon the great anger in your heart.   590

MEDEA   That was not why you didn't tell me; marriage to a foreigner
would not have been prestigious for you in old age.

JASON   Know this well, it was not for the woman's sake
that I have married into royalty,
but, as I said before, I wanted to save you   595
and to breed royal children, brothers to
my sons, to give my house security.

MEDEA   May I never live a prosperous life that's painful,
nor have a kind of wealth that wounds the heart.

JASON   Know you could change this prayer and be more sensible; 600
pray what is good may never seem painful to you,
and that you do not feel unfortunate when you are fortunate.

MEDEA   Mock me, since you have an escape,
while I will leave this land alone.

JASON   You chose that; do not blame somebody else.   605

MEDEA   What did I do? Marry and then betray you?

JASON   You laid unholy curses on the royal family.

MEDEA   I am a curse on your household as well.

JASON   I will not argue with you any more.

Now, if you want some help from my resources   610
for the children or yourself in exile,
speak; I'm prepared to give with no hard feelings,
and send tokens to friends, who will look after you.
You'd be a fool if you refused this, woman;
if you let go of anger you will do much better.   615

MEDEA   I would not use your friends
nor take a thing from you, so do not give;
the gifts of a bad man can do great harm.

JASON   Well, I call upon the gods to witness that
I want to help you and my sons in every way;   620
good things do not please you, but in your arrogance
you push away your friends; it will cause you more pain.

MEDEA   Go; with desire for your newly tamed girl
you're wasting time away from home.

(JASON starts to leave)

Make love to her; perhaps, and with the favour of the gods,   625
your marriage will be such that you will cry in grief.

Exit JASON, left.

Choros 3

WOMEN (A1) Love that comes in great excess does
not grant reputation or excellence;   630
but if Aphrodite comes more gently, there is no other god
who gives such great pleasure.
Mistress, never shoot at me from your golden bow
an inescapable arrow anointed with desire.

(A2) May self-control favour me, the gods' fairest gift;
may fearful Aphrodite not strike me with angry quarrels
and insatiable strife, stunning my heart with lust for
someone else's bed;   640
may she respect all peaceful marriage-beds
when judging with her sharp mind where women make
love.

(B1) My native land, my house, never may I   645
be driven from my city,

living a life of helplessness, hard to survive,
the bitterest of ills.
I'd rather die, be tamed by death   650
before that fate happens to me;
there is no greater suffering
than to cease living in your native land.

(B2) We've seen it, I'm not telling tales
from someone else;   655
no city and no friend will pity you
as you suffer this most terrible fate.
May an ungrateful person be destroyed,   660
one who does not honour family and friends
when he has opened up their hearts and found them pure;
may such a person never be my friend.

Scene 4

Enter AEGEUS, right.

AEGEUS   Medea, be of good fortune; no one can find
    a better way than this to greet a friend.
MEDEA   The same to you too, son of wise Pandion,   665
    Aegeus; what has brought you here?
AEGEUS   I've just come from Apollo's ancient shrine.
MEDEA   Why did you travel to the navel of the earth where oracles
                                                    are sung?
AEGEUS   Searching for how I can have children.
MEDEA   By the gods, are you still childless even now?   670
AEGEUS   Yes, some god's made me childless.
MEDEA   D'you have a wife, or don't you sleep with anyone?
AEGEUS   I have a wife.
MEDEA   What did the prophet-god tell you about children?
AEGEUS   Words too wise for a man to understand.   675
MEDEA   Is it permitted me to hear the oracle from god?
AEGEUS   Definitely, since it needs a person of intelligence.
MEDEA   What was the oracle? Tell me, if it's right for me to hear.
AEGEUS   Not to open the foot of the wineskin –
MEDEA   Before you did what, or came to what land?   680
AEGEUS   – before I went back to my native hearth.
MEDEA   So why have you sailed here?
AEGEUS   There is a man called Pittheus, king of Troezen.

MEDEA	The son of Pelops, so they say, and very pious.
AEGEUS	I want to share the oracle with him. 685
MEDEA	Yes, he's a wise man and experienced in things like this.
AEGEUS	And he's the very dearest of my friends. *(pause)*
MEDEA	Well, may you have good fortune and get what you want.
AEGEUS	Why are your eyes and skin wasted away?
MEDEA	Aegeus, my husband is the worst of all mankind. 690
AEGEUS	What?! Tell me clearly why you're so upset.
MEDEA	Jason is treating me unjustly, with no cause.
AEGEUS	What has he done? Speak more clearly to me.
MEDEA	He has installed a new woman as mistress of my house.
AEGEUS	Surely he would not dare to do something like that? 695
MEDEA	He has; and we, his former friends, are now dishonoured.
AEGEUS	Is he in love, or does he hate sleeping with you?
MEDEA	It's a great love – so great he's been unfaithful to his family.
AEGEUS	Let him go if, as you say, he's a wicked man.
MEDEA	He wanted marriage into royalty. 700
AEGEUS	Who's giving him a wife? Tell me some more.
MEDEA	Creon, the king here in Corinth.
AEGEUS	Then I can understand why you're distressed.
MEDEA	I am destroyed – and worse, they are expelling me.
AEGEUS	Who? This is another, new disaster. 705
MEDEA	Creon is driving me into exile from here.
AEGEUS	And Jason lets this happen? I cannot approve.
MEDEA	He says he doesn't, but he's willing to endure it.

(MEDEA kneels at AEGEUS' feet)

    I entreat you by your beard
    and knees, and am your suppliant;   710
    pity me, pity me in my misfortune,
    do not let me be cast out into wilderness
    but give me refuge in your land and at your hearth.
    If you do this, may the gods fulfil your desire
    for children; also, may you die a happy man.   715
    You don't know what a great find you have made;
    I'll stop you being childless, and I'll make you capable
    of sowing fruitful seed; such are the drugs I know.

AEGEUS	For many reasons I am eager to help you, lady;

    first in reverence for the gods   720
    and then because you tell me I will have children;
    for in this I'm completely helpless now.
    But here is how I stand; if you come to my country,

I'm a just man and I'll receive you as my guest.
But I must tell you this;   725
I am not willing to take you away from here.
However, if you can come to my home
You will remain secure and no one will abduct you.
But you must make your own way out of Corinth;
I do not wish to be blamed by my friends.   730
MEDEA   So shall it be. But if I have a guarantee
of this, all would be well between us.
AEGEUS   Surely you trust me? Or is there some problem?
MEDEA   I trust you; but the house of Pelias is hostile to me,
and of course Creon. If you were constrained by oaths   735
you would not let these enemies take me away;
if we had only just agreed, without an oath sworn by the gods,
you might become their friend, and yield
to their requests; for I am weak,
and they are wealthy, live the life of royalty.   740
AEGEUS   You've shown great foresight, and
if you want this, I'm willing to comply.
It will be safer for me too,
if I have some excuse to show your enemies,
and you'll be more secure. So name your gods.   745
MEDEA   Swear by the Earth and by my grandfather the Sun
and the whole race of the immortals.
AEGEUS   To do or not to do what? Speak.
MEDEA   Never to expel me from your land,
nor, if an enemy of mine attempts   750
to take me, willingly to let me go.
AEGEUS   I swear by Earth and by the bright light of the Sun
and all the gods to honour what you have just said.
MEDEA   That's fine. What would you suffer if you did not
                        keep your oath?
AEGEUS   What happens to all impious men.   755
MEDEA   And so farewell. This is all good,
and I will come to Athens just as soon as possible,
when I have done what I intend and have got what I want.
WOMEN   May Hermes god of travellers
take you safe home, and may you achieve   760
all you desire,
since, Aegeus, I think you're
a noble man.

Exit AEGEUS, right. Enter Medea's ATTENDANT from the house.

MEDEA   Oh Zeus, Justice of Zeus and radiance of the Sun,
        now, friends, I will have graceful victory over my
                                    antagonists   765
    and we have started on the road.
    There is now hope my enemies will pay the penalty.
    for where I was in very great distress
    this man has come, the safe harbour my plans require,
    and I will moor my stern-cable to him   770
    when I go to the city of Athena.

    Now I will tell you all my plans;
    But you won't like the words I say.
    I'll send one of my servants who will ask
    Jason to come and see me.   775
    And when he comes I'll speak soft words to him –
    that I agree with him and that his royal marriage,
    though betraying me, is sensible,
    both advantageous and a good decision.
    I shall then beg him for our sons to stay;   780
    I won't be leaving them in hostile territory,   781
    but so I can kill the king's daughter by deceit. 783
    For I will send them bringing presents in their hands – 784
    a delicate robe and a wreath made out of gold;   786
    and if she takes the finery and puts it round her skin,
    she'll perish gruesomely, and anyone who touches her –
    such are the poisons with which I'll anoint the gifts.

    That is enough about this plan. But then   790
    I'm miserable about what I must do.
    I have to kill my children;
    no one will take them from my hands.
    And when I have destroyed the house of Jason,
    I will depart this land, escaping from the murder 795
    of my dearest children, having endured this utterly unholy act.
    For it's not tolerable, friends, if enemies can laugh at you. 797
    I made a terrible mistake once, when I fled from my 800
    ancestral halls, persuaded by the words of a Greek man –
    who will now with god's help pay me the penalty.
    For he will never see the children whom he had

by me, nor will he father children from
his brand-new bride, since she, a wicked woman, must die   805
wickedly, through my poisons' power.
Let no one think me insignificant or weak,
or gentle – I am quite the opposite;
a heavy burden on my enemies and a great help to my friends;
people like this live the most glorious life.   810

1 WOMAN   Since you have shared this plan with us,
I want to help you and uphold the laws
that govern humans; I say you must not do this.

MEDEA   It can't be otherwise. I'll pardon you for what you've said
because you haven't suffered evil like I have.   815

1 WOMAN   Will you, a woman, dare to kill your offspring?

MEDEA   Yes; that's the best way I can make my husband suffer.

1 WOMAN   But you would then be the most wretched of women.

MEDEA   So let it be; all words of compromise are now superfluous.
(To an ATTENDANT)
Go and fetch Jason;   820
I use you for all that requires a special trust.
You will say nothing of what I have planned,
if you are on your mistress' side, and you were born a woman.

Exit ATTENDANT, left; exit MEDEA into the house.

Choros 4

WOMEN   (A1) Athenians are prosperous from long ago,
and children of the blessed gods.   825
Their land is sacred and has never been conquered;
they feed themselves on their most famous wisdom,
always stepping with grace through their pure air,   830
where men say the nine Muses of Pieria
created blonde-haired Harmony.

(A2) And they proclaim too that upon the banks   835
of beautifully flowing Cēphisus Aphrodite draws water
and wafts down on the land sweet-blowing,
gentle breezes; she always adorns her hair   840
with fragrant roses, when she's sending out
Eros and his companions to be partners with
Wisdom, and help all kinds of excellence.   845

(B1) How can this city, home of sacred rivers,
which gives safe escort to its friends,

receive you, murderess of children,
impious, to live inside its halls? 850
Think about the blow struck against them,
think about the slaughter you take on yourself.
I implore and supplicate you, absolutely and in every
way,
don't kill your children. 855

(B2) Where will you get the daring
for your hand and heart to do
this dreadful thing?
How can you look upon 860
your children's fate with tearless eyes
and kill them? When they kneel as suppliants
you won't be able to defile your hand
with their blood, with a steadfast heart. 865

Scene 5

Enter JASON, left, followed by MEDEA'S ATTENDANT.
Enter MEDEA from the house.

JASON   You summoned me; I've come. Although you hate me,
you weren't wrong; I am here to listen.
What new thing do you want of me, woman?
MEDEA   Jason, I beg you to forgive
the things I said; it would be right for you 870
to tolerate my anger, since we were once so much in love.
I had an inner conversation, and then I accused myself:
'Stupid woman, why am I so mad
and treating badly those who wish me well?
I've made myself an enemy to those who rule this land 875
and to my husband, who is doing what is best for us
in marrying a princess and creating brothers
for my children. Should I not let this anger go?
What's wrong with me? The gods are looking after me.
Do I not know that I have children, and we will be exiled 880
from this land and in much need of friends?'
I thought this through, and recognized that I'd
been very thoughtless and had raged for nothing.
So now I praise you, and I think you're very wise
to add this marriage-bond to us – it's I who lost my wits. 885
I should have taken part in all those plans

and helped you, and stood by the marriage-bed
to take delight in caring for your bride.
But we are what we are – I will not say we're bad –
we women; it would be very wrong for you to be like us,   890
or to respond to foolish words with foolishness.
I ask for pardon and admit that I was quite wrong then,
but I have now thought better.

Children, come here, leave the house,
(Enter SONS with TUTOR, from the house)

come here, embrace your father, talk to him   895
with me; you must forget our former enmity
for this dear man just like your mother does;
for we now have a truce and all anger has gone.
Take his right hand.
(The SONS do this)
                              Oh, how I think of hidden evils.   900
My children, will you live for a long time
and hold out your dear arms like this? I am wretched,
near to tears and full of fear.
At last I have ended my strife with your father
and I am weeping at this tender sight.   905
1 WOMAN   I too have fresh tears in my eyes; I hope no greater trouble
comes than what we have already.
JASON   Lady, I praise this, and I don't blame you for what is past;
it's natural for women to get angry when
another marriage has been smuggled in the house.   910
But your feelings have now changed for the better.
At last you've recognized the winning plan;
this is the action of a woman who is sensible.
As for you, children, your father has taken thought
and with the gods has given great security to you.   915
I think that in this land of Corinth you will be
among the first of men, together with your brothers.
Grow and prosper; all the rest your father will arrange,
with whichever god is well disposed to us.
I hope to see you thrive and reach the goal   920
of young manhood, becoming stronger than my enemies.

Woman, why do you wet your eyes with glistening tears,
turning your white cheek away,
and don't receive this speech of mine with joy?

MEDEA	It's nothing. I was just thinking about these boys.	925
JASON	Be confident. I will arrange all well for them.	
MEDEA	I will. I will not disobey your words;	

women are feeble and are prone to tears.

JASON	But why do you grieve so much for these boys?	
MEDEA	I gave birth to them; and when you prayed	
	that they would live,	930

pity came on me fearing that this may not happen.

But as to why you came to speak to me,
some things have been said, but I must mention one more.
The ruler of this land is sending me away
(and that is best for me, I fully recognize, 935
not to be in your way or that of the royal family;
for they think I am hostile to their house).
So I'll depart into exile;
but please beg Creon that your sons don't have to go,
and he will let you bring them up. 940

JASON	I see that I must try, but I don't know if I can persuade him.	
MEDEA	You could ask your wife to beg her father	

if the boys can be allowed to stay.

JASON	A great idea! And I am sure I will persuade her,	
	If she is like other women.	945
MEDEA	I will help you with this;	

I'll send her gifts which men count as the best
of all that exist in the world – I know that well;
a delicate robe and a wreath made out of gold.
The boys will take them. Let one of my 950
attendants bring this finery, quick as you can.

(*Exit ATTENDANT into the house*)

She will be fortunate in many thousand ways
having in you a husband who is excellent
and in obtaining finery which once the Sun
My grandfather gave to his family. 955

(*Re-enter ATTENDANT with gifts in two boxes*)

Boys, take these marriage-gifts,
and give them to the happy princess-bride;
she will have faultless presents.

JASON	Why, foolish woman, d'you give these away?	
	D'you think the royal palace short of robes	960

or gold? Keep these things, do not give them.
If my wife thinks well of me,

I'm sure she will consider that rather than gifts.

MEDEA   Don't tell me that; it's said that gifts persuade even the gods;
and gold is better than a thousand words.   965
She has good fortune, a god raises her on high,
she's young and powerful; and for my sons' release from exile
I'd give not just gold but my life.

Exit JASON, left.

Children, go to the wealthy house,
and beg my mistress, your father's new wife,   970
not to be exiled, giving her this finery.
It's most important that you place these gifts
in her own hands. Go quickly; succeed, and bring me,
your mother, the good news of what I want.   975

Exeunt TUTOR and SONS, left. Exit ATTENDANT into the house.

Choros 5

WOMEN   (A1) Now I have no more hope for the children,
None at all; they are already going to their deaths.
The bride, unfortunate, will be destroyed
when she receives the golden headband;
She herself will place on her blonde hair   980
The finery of Hades.

(A2) Their divine grace and gleam will persuade her to wear
the robe and golden crown;
she will adorn herself for marriage to death.   985
Such is the trap and deadly fate
into which she, unfortunate, will fall; and she
will not escape destruction.

(B1) But you, the wretched and ill-married son-in-law   990
of kings, in ignorance you're bringing miserable death
to your sons and your wife; unfortunate,
how far you have swerved from your destiny.   995

(B2) Now I am truly sorry for your grief, unhappy mother
of these children, who will slaughter them
because of your own marriage-bed,
which your husband deserted lawlessly,   1000
and sleeps now with somebody else.

Scene 6

Enter BOYS and TUTOR, left.

TUTOR   Mistress, here are your children freed from exile;
   the princess-bride gladly received into her hands
   Your gifts; all is peace there for the boys.
   Ah!
   Why do you stand there so upset, when you are fortunate?   1005
MEDEA *Aiai!*
TUTOR This does not match up with my news.   1008
MEDEA *Aiai!*
TUTOR   Do I not know of some misfortune?
     Was I wrong in thinking that my news is good?   1010
MEDEA You've told me what you've told me. You've
          done nothing wrong.
TUTOR Then why are you downcast and crying?
MEDEA I have no other choice, old man; the gods and I
   have done this – and we were completely wrong.
TUTOR Be confident; your sons will bring you back.   1015
MEDEA I'm desperate; I won't return – and I'll bring others down.
TUTOR You're not the only one who's been deprived of children;
   being but mortal, we must bear misfortune lightly.
MEDEA I'll do that; you must go inside
   and provide for the children what they need today.   1020

(*Exit TUTOR into the house*)

   Oh my children, you still have a city and a home
   in which, leaving poor me, you'll live
   always without a mother;
   I shall go to another land an exile long before
   I can rejoice in you and see you prosperous,   1025
   before I can adorn your splendid ritual baths, your
          wives and marriage-beds
   and lift the torch on high.
   I'm miserable because of what I've dared to do.
   I've brought you up in vain, my children, and
   in vain I've worked for you, been worn out by my pain,   1030
   suffering the agony of childbirth for nothing.
   Once I, unhappy one, had many hopes for you,

that you would tend me in old age
and lay my corpse out with your hands when I am dead,
the fate envied by everyone; now that sweet thought   1035
has been destroyed. I will be deprived of you
and live a long and wretched, painful life –
and your dear eyes will never see your mother,
as you pass to another form of life.

Oh! Oh! Why do you look at me, my sons?   1040
Why do you smile the last of all your smiles?
Aiai! What shall I do? Women, my brave resolve is gone
as I look on the bright eyes of my sons.
I cannot! Farewell my former plans;
I'll take my children with me, leaving here.   1045
Why should I, angry with their father, by their fate
myself be burdened with this second wrong?
No, I won't. Farewell my plans.

And yet, what's wrong with me? Do I want to let
my enemies go without punishment, so I become
                              a laughingstock?   1050
I must have courage. It would be sheer cowardice
to let soft words into my mind.   1052
If anyone is ritually restrained   1054
from presence at my sacrifice,
that is their concern; my hand will not be weak.   1055
Everything's done; there will be no escape;   1064
the royal bride is dying with the crown   1065
upon her head, and in the robe; of that I'm sure.
But, since I am embarked on a most wretched road,
and I will send these on one even worse,
I want to talk to my children; sons, please give
me your right hands to kiss.   1070
Oh dearest hand, oh dearest mouth to me,
and noble form and faces of my children,
may you be fortunate – but somewhere else; your father
has removed all joy from here. Oh sweet embrace,
oh soft skin and sweet breath of children.   1075
Go, go; I can no longer look at you,
but am consumed by sufferings.

(*Exeunt SONS into the house*)

I know how great a crime I'm going to commit,
but anger has control over my plans –
anger, which is the greatest cause of human pain.   1080

Choral interlude

WOMEN   Often before I have engaged
        in subtler thoughts, and struggled
        with ideas larger than women
        are supposed to grapple with.
        But we too have a muse   1085
        who shares things with us because we are wise
        – not with all women, but with few
        (perhaps you would find one among many);
        we females have some talents.
        And I say people who have no   1090
        experience and no children
        are far more happy than
        those who have them.
        Being without experience,
        they do not find out if it's sweet   1095
        or painful to have children –
        and they avoid many troubles.
        But as for those who have the joy
        of children in their house, I see them
        exhausted all the time with cares,   1100
        first how they can bring up their children well
        and leave a livelihood to them;
        then after that they will be working hard
        for children who will turn out good or bad –
        that is unknown.
        And then I say there is one more bad thing   1105
        given to mortals – it's the worst of all;
        suppose they've found sufficient means to live
        and their children have grown up
        and turn out to be good; if a god sees fit
        Death goes down to Hades,   1110
        taking the bodies of the children.
        What is the reason why the gods
        on top of other torments cast
        upon us this intolerable pain
        for having children?   1115

Scene 7

MEDEA   I have long waited anxiously
    to find out what has happened in the palace.
    Now I see one of Jason's men
    coming here. He is out of breath –
    that shows he has bad news.   1120

Enter MESSENGER, left.

MESSENGER   Medea, you must flee, flee   1122
    by land or sea.
MEDEA   Why should I have to flee?
MESSENGER   The princess has just perished,   1125
    and her father too, Creon, because of your poisons.
MEDEA   Most beautiful of news, and you will be
    forever friend and benefactor to me.
MESSENGER   What are you saying? Are you mad or sane, woman?
    You have outrageously defiled the royal house,   1130
    and you rejoice to hear such things and have no fear?
MEDEA   I've something I could say against
    your words. But do not hurry, friend;
    tell me – how did they die? You will give me
    twice the pleasure, if they perished horribly.   1135
MESSENGER   When your two children came
    together with their father to the bridal house,
    we servants who had sympathized with your troubles
    rejoiced; and at once many people said
    you and your husband had made peace.   1140
    Some kissed the hands, others the blond hair
    of your two sons; and I myself, delighted,
    followed the children to the women's room.
    The mistress whom we honour now instead of you
    before she saw the pair of children   1145
    looked with an eager, loving eye at Jason;
    but then she veiled her eyes
    and turned her white cheek so as not to look,
    disgusted by the children's entry. Your husband
    soothed the girl's rage and temper,   1150
    saying this: 'Do not be hostile to our friends,
    please cease your anger and turn back your face.
    Consider that your husband's friends are yours as well;

will you receive these gifts and ask your father not
to send these children into exile, for my sake?'   1155
When she saw the presents, she did not refuse
but agreed fully with her husband, and before
your children and their father had gone far,
she took the multicoloured robe and wrapped it round herself,
then placed the golden crown upon her locks   1160
and with a mirror she arranged her hair,
smiling at the lifeless image of her form.
She got up from her throne and walked around the room,
taking light steps on her white feet,
delighting in her gifts, and many, many times   1165
looking back to see how the robe flowed to her heel.

But then we saw a terrifying sight;
her skin began to change, she staggered sideways,
and only just was able to
sit on the throne and not fall to the ground.   1170
One old serving woman, thinking I suppose
the ecstasy of Pan or of some other god had come,
Raised a glad cry; but then she saw white foam
spewing from the girl's mouth, and her eyes
stood out from their sockets, and there was no blood
              in her flesh.   1175
Then instead of joyful song there was a huge outcry of grief.
At once a slave went to her father's rooms,
another to her newlywed husband,
telling what had happened to the bride; and the whole house
resounded with the sound of rushing feet.   1180
A swift runner would have got to the end
of a two hundred metre race,
before she broke her silence and with open eyes
stirred, wretched girl, and cried aloud.
For two pains were attacking her at once;   1185
the wreath of gold around her head
let out a stream of all-consuming fire,
and the fine robe, gift from your sons,
devoured the white flesh of the girl fated to suffer.
She got up from her throne and fled on fire,   1190
shaking her head and hair this way and that,
trying to take off the crown; but the golden band
held firm, and when she shook her hair the fire

burned twice as fiercely.
She fell onto the floor, overcome by this disaster;   1195
almost no one except her father would have recognized her.
You could not see the shape her eyes had been,
nor her once well-formed face, as blood dripped from
the top of her head, blended with the fire;
and the flesh melted away from her bones like sap from
                                    a pine tree   1200
due to the hidden jaws of your poisons –
a terrifying sight. No one dared to touch
the corpse; we had what happened as our guide.
Her wretched father, ignorant of the disaster,
suddenly came into the room and fell upon the corpse.   1205
At once he cried out and embraced her with his hands
and kissed her, saying: 'My poor daughter,
what god's destroyed you horribly?
Who's made this old man, one foot in the grave,
bereft of you? Alas, may I die with you, child'.   1210
And when he had ceased his laments,
he tried to get up with his agèd body,
but he was held like ivy on the shoots of laurel
by her light robe, and then there was an awful wrestling- match.
He wanted to stand up,   1215
but she held him tightly; if he tried force,
he tore the old flesh off his bones.
In time the poor unfortunate was snuffed right out
and died; he could no longer fight against his fate.
There are two corpses – an old father and his daughter   1220
lie together; a disaster to provoke weeping.

Let your affairs be left out of my tale;
you'll know yourself what punishment will fall on you.
Not for the first time, I consider mortal life a mere shadow;
I would not hesitate to say that those   1225
who are thought to be wise and deft with words
incur the greatest charge – of foolishness.
No human being's ever favoured by the gods;
when wealth flows in, someone may be more prosperous
than others; but still, he's not then happy.   1230

Exit MESSENGER, left.

1 WOMAN   It seems that on this day the god
    has imposed many sufferings on Jason – and justly so.   1232
MEDEA   My friends, I have decided that I must   1236
    kill the children at once and then leave here.
    I must not let delay give the boys over
    to be slaughtered by an enemy.
    They have to die; and since they must,   1240
    I who gave birth to them shall kill them.

    Arm yourself, my heart; why do I delay
    committing this awful but necessary crime?
    Come, desperate hand, take up the sword,
    take it, and creep to where the misery of life begins.   1245
    Don't weaken; don't remember your children,
    how they are very dear, how you gave birth to them, but just
    for this short day forget your sons; then
    you can lament them. Even though you kill them,
    they were born dear to you. I am unfortunate.   1250

Exit MEDEA into the house.

Choros 6

WOMEN (A1) Oh Earth and radiant light of Sun,
           look, look at this
           accursèd woman now, before her bloody,
           kindred-murdering hand strikes down
           her two children;
           for she was born of your gold lineage,   1255
           and it is fearful for the blood of gods
           to fall onto the earth shed by the hands of men.
           Divine Light, stop her, hold her back,
           drive this wretched, bloodstained Fury
           out of the house.   1260

    (A2) In vain the toil of raising children's lost;
           in vain you bore these loved ones, and
           came through the hostile passageway
           Between the dark-blue Clashing Rocks.
           Miserable woman, why has this mad rage   1265
           fallen on you and made you pile
                        frenzied murder upon murder?

Pollution caused by kindred murder's terrible;
it brings onto the killers
sufferings that match their crimes,
woes falling from the gods upon the house.   1270

BOY (*inside the house*)   Help!   1270a

WOMEN (B1)   D'you hear the children crying out?   1273
             Wretched, ill-fated woman.   1274
BOY 1   Oh, what shall I do? How can I escape my mother's
                                              hands?   1271
BOY 2   I do not know, dear brother; we are done for.   1272
WOMEN   Shall I go inside? I think we should   1275
             stop her from murdering her children.
BOY 1   Yes by the gods, help us; we need you. *(screams)*
BOY 2   She has us caught in the trap of her sword. *(screams)*
WOMEN   Wretched woman, you were a rock or iron   1280
             to kill with your own fateful kindred hand
             the children whom you bore.

        (B2) I've heard of one and only one
              woman before who killed her children –
              Ino, maddened by the gods,
              when Zeus' consort sent her wandering from home.   1285
              The wretched one fell in the sea,
              an impious murderess of her sons,
              putting her foot over a cliff,
              and died together with her two children.
              What terror's now impossible?   1290
              Oh marriage-bed of women, full of pain,
              what evils you have done to humankind!

Scene 8 (finale)

Enter JASON, left.

JASON   You women who are standing here,
        is she who did these frightful crimes,
        Medea, in the house or has she fled?   1295
        She'll have to hide herself beneath the earth
        or take wing and fly up into the sky,
        if she is not to pay the royal house for what she's done.
        Did she think she could kill the rulers of this land

and then escape without a penalty?   1300
But I am not thinking about her so much as my sons;
the victims will give her due punishment;
but I have come to save the children's lives,
fearing the royals' relatives will do them harm,
exacting vengeance for their mother's impious crime.   1305

1 WOMAN   Jason, poor man, you do not know
what you have suffered, or you would not have said this.

JASON   What is it? Does she want to kill me too?

1 WOMAN   Your children are dead, slain by their own mother.

JASON   No! What do you mean? Woman, you have
                                              destroyed me.   1310

1 WOMAN   You must accept that you have no more children.

JASON   Where did she kill them? Outdoors or inside?

1 WOMAN   Open the doors, and you will see your dead children.

JASON   Servants, undo the bolts as fast as possible,
open the doors, so I can see this double crime.   1315

Enter MEDEA on high.

MEDEA   Why are you shaking and trying to force the doors   1317
to find the bodies and myself, who did the deed?
Stop wasting labour; if you need me,
speak if you want something; but you won't get
                                              your hands on me.   1320
Such is this chariot my grandfather the Sun
has given me, protection from all hostile hands.

JASON   You despicable creature, woman hated most
by gods and men and the whole human race,
you dared to put your own sons to the sword –   1325
you, their mother – and you have destroyed me, childless.
You've done this, yet you look upon the sun
and earth, after daring this most impious act?
I hope you die! I am wise now, and I was foolish then
when I brought you from your home in a barbarous land   1330
to live in Greece, a great evil, and traitress
to your father and the land that nurtured you.
The gods have brought your vengeance down on me as well;
for you killed your own brother by the hearth
before you came on board the glorious ship Argo.   1335
That was just the beginning; when you had married me
and bore me children, you destroyed them,
all because of sexual jealousy.

No Greek woman would have dared to do this,
but I preferred to marry you instead of one,   1340
a hateful union which has destroyed me.
You are a lioness, no woman, more savage
in your nature than Etruscan Scylla.
Not even with thousands of reproaches could I bite you;
such is the daring deep inside your soul.   1345
Go to hell, doer of shameful deeds and butcher of your children.
It is for me to mourn my fate;
I do not have enjoyment of my new marriage,
and I will not have living children to talk to
whom I fathered and brought up – all is lost.   1350

MEDEA   I could have spoken at length in reply to this –
but Zeus the Father knows what I have done for you
                              and what you've done.
You were not going to dishonour my bed and enjoy
a joyful life laughing at me, nor was the princess.   1355
And Creon, who gave you that marriage, never was
going to cast me out without revenge.
That's that; and if you want you can call me a lioness,
or Scylla who inhabits an Etruscan rock;
for I've attacked your heart as you deserve.   1360

JASON   You yourself suffer and share in the misery.

MEDEA   Know this; the pain is worthwhile, if you cannot laugh at me.

JASON   Children, how bad a mother you have had.

MEDEA   Children, you died because your father is diseased.

JASON   It was not *my* right hand that killed them   1365

MEDEA   No, it was your arrogance and your new wedding.

JASON   You thought it right to kill them just because of sex?

MEDEA   D'you think that is a small affliction for a woman?

JASON   For one who's self-controlled; but everything about you's evil.

MEDEA   These boys are dead; and that will bite at you.   1370

JASON   These boys will be avengers on your head.

MEDEA   The gods know who began these sufferings.

JASON   At least they know of your disgusting mind.

MEDEA   Hate me; I loathe your bitter voice.

JASON   And I yours; but our parting will be easy.   1375

MEDEA   How? What shall I do? I really want that too.

JASON   Allow me to bury these bodies and mourn over them.

MEDEA   No; I shall bury them with my own hand.
I'll take them to the sacred precinct of Hera Acraia
so that none of their enemies can mutilate the dead

by tearing down their tombs. Then on this land of Sisyphus 1380
I will bestow a sacred feast and future rites
because of this impious death.
I myself am going to the land of the Athenians;
I'll live with Aegeus, son of Pandion. 1385
You, as is right, will die an ignominious death
struck on the head by an old timber of the ship Argo,
seeing a bitter ending to your marriage with me.

JASON   May the avenging Fury of the children and Justice
        destroy you. 1390

MEDEA   What god or other power will listen to you,
        a man who breaks oaths and deceives his friends?

JASON   You are a loathsome murderess.

MEDEA   Go to your house and bury your wife.

JASON   I go, deprived of my children. 1395

MEDEA   You are not really mourning yet; wait for old age.

JASON   Oh dearest children –

MEDEA   To their mother, not to you.

JASON   And then you killed them?

MEDEA   Yes, to cause you pain.

JASON   Oh, I'm miserable; how I wish that I could kiss
        the dear mouths of my children. 1400

MEDEA   Now you call out to them, now you greet them,
        When you'd pushed them away.

JASON   By the gods,
        let me touch the soft skin of my children.

MEDEA   No; you speak uselessly.

Exit MEDEA.

JASON   Zeus, do you hear how I'm deprived 1405
        and what I suffer from this horrible
        child-murderer and lioness?
        But I will do all that I can
        to mourn for them and appeal to the gods,
        calling the divine powers to witness how 1410
        you killed my children and did not allow
        me to touch them or bury their dead bodies.
        How I wish I'd never fathered them
        to see them killed by you.

Exit JASON, left.

WOMEN   Zeus on Olympus ordains many things,   1415
                 and gods achieve much that surprises us.
                 What we thought would happen didn't,
                 and the god found a way for unimaginable deeds;
                 That's how this story ends.

Exeunt WOMEN, left.

The aftermath

In Troezen, Pittheus realized the meaning of the oracle and got Aegeus drunk so that he slept with Pittheus' daughter Aethra. Their offspring was to become the great Athenian hero Theseus.

Medea made her way to Athens and married Aegeus. According to one version of the story, she had a son by him called Medus; another version has Medea conceive Medus by a barbarian father after she had departed from Athens.

There is a legend, not necessarily current in Euripides' time, that Medea had to flee because when Theseus arrived in Athens as a grown young man, she tried to poison him, but Aegeus recognized him as his son just in time and prevented him from drinking the poisoned drink.

Medea travelled east to the area now known as Iran and Syria; she and her son Medus founded and ruled the nation of the Medes there.

Translation notes

20   Literally 'been dishonoured' – but Medea's loss of *timē* is so central to the play that this expansion gives it due emphasis on its first occurrence.

38–43   A later actor or director inserted here some lines which anticipate all too obviously what is going to happen later in the play.

65   Statements of supplication (e.g. 'by your knees') are sometimes very important – as, for example, for Medea with Creon and Aegeus later in this play and for Jason when he swore his oaths to her (495–7), but in this line, the Nurse's invocation 'By your beard' has very little significance, and I have decided to omit it.

87   A spurious line which damages the sense of the speech has been cut.

111, 144, etc. *Aiai!* Greek has several exclamations of grief or other high emotion. Most of them (*oimoi, pheu*, etc.) sound incongruous when transcribed in an otherwise English translation (Gregory McCart's 1998 version of *Medea* leaves them all untranslated, and Rayor 2013 uses *oimoi* and *puh* [sic]), but I have tested *Aiai* in productions of Sophocles' *Aias* (*Ajax*), where the hero reflects on the tragic similarity of his name to this cry of grief, and of Theocritus' poem 2, *Love Magic* – as well of course as in the performances of this translation of *Medea*. And this visceral sound really works on the modern stage.

136   In the Greek, 'two-doored house'. But I omit the adjectival phrase as distracting for a modern audience.

246   A spurious line which damages the sense of the speech has been cut.

262   A spurious line which damages the sense of the speech has been cut.

304   A line mistakenly copied here from 808 has been omitted.

334   This line is corrupt in the manuscripts; I translate a plausible reconstruction since the sense is clear.

DOI: 10.4324/9781003215844-3

355–6   Some scholars delete these two lines, but they have been ably defended by Mastronade (2002: 230).

361   A scribe who misunderstood the Greek added a superfluous verb.

397   In its original position, this parenthesis makes it almost impossible for an actress to keep the continuity of the sentence 395–8. Transposing 398 and 397 yields a much more playable outcome.

468   This line is deleted by most editors since it is identical to 1340. But it has a point here just as well as there, and its omission cuts off Medea's rhetorical build-up without a proper climax.

725–9   A papyrus gives a different order for these lines, and several editors have deleted 725–6 and accepted a rearrangement of 727–9. Like Page (1938) and Maravela-Solbakk (2008), I see every reason to let the manuscript text stand. Aegeus needs to emphasize this crucial point.

782   Editors agree that a spurious line has been inserted here.

785   Editors agree that a spurious line has been inserted here.

798–9   Two interpolated lines omitted.

856–9   The manuscript text of the Greek here is deeply corrupt, and this translation like all others guesses what Euripides might have written.

949   This line is an exact repetition of 786, often deleted here as such. But it is essential, as otherwise, Jason will not know what the gifts are – and he clearly does at 960–1.

1006–7   Two superfluous, repetitive lines have been deleted.

1053   'Children, go inside the house'. This is premature; she has yet to take their hands and embrace them before she sends them in. I think this is one more sign of incompetent interpolation into this speech (see following).

1057–63
   Ah, Ah!
   My heart, do not do this.
   Wretched woman, let them spare your children;
   They will live and give you joy.
   By the avenging Furies of the underworld,
   It will not happen that I'll let my enemies 1060
   Possess my children and abuse them. 1061
   They have to die; and since they must, 1062 = 1240
   I who gave birth to them shall kill them. 1063 = 1241

   Most of 1056–61 are bad Greek verses, and they are totally incoherent as part of Medea's thought-processes in the monologue.

Accordingly, they have been rejected by most editors and commentators (and 1062–3, utterly impossible with the children present, were imported from 1240–1); the whole of 1056–63 must be regarded, as Mossman argues (2011: 324–6), as an actor's interpolation (*pace* e.g. Seidensticker 1990; Michelini 1989). Some commentators (cf. esp. Reeve 1972) have gone even further and deleted the whole of 1056 to 1080; Diggle followed him in the Oxford Classical Text (1984). Verses 1064–80 are probably genuine Euripides – they are certainly written in his style; the other, much less likely possibility is that the passage was added later, together with 1056–63, to milk the emotion of Medea's last encounter with the children before killing them.

1078–80   These three lines have been extensively discussed, and variously interpreted, since antiquity. Mossman (2011) recommends their deletion. But I see no problem if they are translated as in this version.

1121   A melodramatic opening line for the Messenger is an obvious interpolation.

1221   This line is corrupt in the Greek, and the sense given here is approximate.

1233–5   Three sentimental lines focusing on the princess's fate have been interpolated by a later actor/director.

1260   The last two words of this line are deeply corrupted in the manuscripts; what Euripides wrote cannot be reconstructed, and no attempt is made in this translation.

1316   'Two children dead – and I will punish her' is unlikely to be genuine.

1362   Possibly 'Know this; it removes the pain' (the Greek is ambiguous). But I prefer the translation given in my text.

1415–19   These closing lines are identical except for 1415 with the closing lines of several other surviving plays of Euripides. Some editors recommend their deletion. But the choros in Greek tragedy never exits in silence, without a closing lyric stanza, unless there is good reason (cf. Aeschylus, *Agamemnon*, where the ending is a snarling exchange of insults between Aigisthos and the Elders), and these lines, with the unique first line 'Zeus on Olympus ordains many things', have a particular appropriateness to this play, in which the power of Zeus to punish an oath-breaker has been demonstrated, and the Women of Corinth, together with the audience, have been taken on a roller-coaster of suspense as to what will happen next at every phase of the action – or more precisely, what Medea will do next.

Theatrical commentary

Performing *Medea* on a stage with an end-on audience

After an introduction, this commentary first outlines the content of each Scene and Choros and then discusses, with reference to our successful 2021 research production in Newcastle Australia, some of the strategies that can be adopted to make this play into a gripping contemporary experience in an end-on theatre. Wider issues, such as how in general to approach acting, character and the choros in Greek tragedy and comedy, are treated in my book *Staging Greek Drama: A Practical Guide for Directors, Actors and Drama Students.*[1]

The unwritten rules of the end-on modern space are very different from those of the theatre in which *Medea* was first performed. In the ancient Greek theatre, the audience surrounded the action on three sides, so the rear half of the *orchēstra* gave characters more power than the front half because when an actor advanced beyond the centre line, progressively fewer members of the audience could see the front of his mask. In the end-on theatre, these priorities are reversed; the front of the stage is more powerful, except when someone enters from the rear and briefly 'upstages' characters already onstage further forward. Accordingly, the movements have to be worked through for the new space, in ways which often contradict what the playwright might originally have created.

Whatever its shape, the performance space for a Greek drama should have entries from left and right, and through the doors of a building upstage, as in the original Theatre of Dionysus; this makes production easy and clear, while sets which do not conform to this requirement will cause confusion as to the direction from which a character is coming into the playing area. In this play, the scene is set in front of Medea's house in Corinth; almost all entries are either from that house or from the stage left entrance leading to downtown Corinth and the royal palace. The sole exception is the arrival and departure of Aegeus, who comes from Delphi and leaves for

DOI: 10.4324/9781003215844-4

Troezen – therefore via the stage right entrance, as he is coming from and going to destinations other than the city of Corinth.

The shape of the modern theatre building encourages watching a play as a 'peep show', with interior scenes often created by three-walled box sets and visible to the darkened audience through the 'fourth wall', but the performance space for a Greek drama always represents an outdoor meeting-place. In this play, it is an area outside Medea's house in which the public – and authority, in the person of Creon – encounters the private. Accordingly, people who come into it from the house, especially Medea herself, do so in the knowledge that they are moving out into a public arena. This fact helps, in the end-on theatre, to break down the 'fourth wall'; the audience is readily made part of the public that is addressed and included, and in our production, this was assisted by raising the house lights for some particular sections of the play (see the following).

Our production of *Medea* took place on a smallish end-on stage, seven metres wide, with no thrust, in a theatre with a capacity of 140 seats. The set consisted of the façade of a house upstage, with one central set of double doors and a window. (To facilitate swift entries from and exits to the interior, the doors were fitted with two-way hinges. This is a simple practical measure which is really useful when staging Greek tragedy and comedy.) The window had a blind behind it but no glass so that the offstage dialogue which is important in this play – Medea's outcries in Scene 1 and Choros 1, and the boys' cries for help and death-shrieks during Choros 6 – could be heard clearly. There was also a raised platform upstage right, for Medea's final appearance.

In front of the façade, there was a playing space seven metres wide and five metres deep. Two benches were placed at the extreme right and left, very near the front edge of the stage; they were set on a diagonal facing into the playing area. These were for the Women of Corinth to sit on when not taking part in the action, facing away from the audience so that they would not pull focus. There were four Women, two on each side, and as all the odes in this play after Choros 1 are four stanzas long, it was possible to distribute the parts evenly. Music (an electronic composition) was only heard after the sinister opening flourish when Euripides' original text was in lyric metres, and all choros lines were spoken over this music by individuals, except the last line of the play ('that's how this story ends'), which was declaimed in unison.

This tight performance space, together with the modern dress costumes and a much-reduced choros speaking as individuals, transformed *Medea* from a spectacle for a vast open-air theatre with a 20-metre square playing area into a contemporary chamber play confined between the two black side walls of the stage and the façade of Medea's house. Our aim was to foster an intensity at least as powerful as that of one of Strindberg's dramas of domestic conflict, by a constant flow between Scenes and Choroses and a steady build-up to and beyond the climactic murder of the children. Intimate contact was possible in this smallish space – for example, when one of the Women tries to console Medea:

> Your sufferings have made you miserable,
> unhappy woman;
> where will you turn? What friend,
> what house, what land will save you from your troubles?
> The gods have thrown you, Medea,
> into a surge of troubles that can't be escaped.
>
> (358–63)

It was both possible and desirable for the Woman speaking this stanza to approach Medea, touch her and help her to her feet. (A similar tactic was used at 996ff., and since the same individual spoke both of these stanzas, as well as the verdict on Jason at 576–8, she was marked out as even more sympathetic to Medea than the other three Women.)

At the first rehearsal, I told the actors, 'Greek tragedy is demanding. You are exposed; in front of a façade, with no props and no furniture in which to orient yourself, lots of dialogue and some long speeches. And there are no wasted words or casual conversation; *Medea* is full on from the first line to the last. It is totally different from acting in a modern play. But I hope and expect that you will thrive on the challenge. I want our *Medea* to thrill and disturb the audiences'. In a small- to medium-sized theatre, actors can draw on acting techniques learnt in working on modern realistic theatre, provided that they are adapted to the different demands and high level of passion in a Greek tragedy. (There is however no subtext in Greek tragedy. Characters say what they mean and mean what they say, except of course when speaking ironically or in scenes of deception.) It is very important to train all the actors, both soloists and choros, to be aware of the sound, rhythm and near-constant flow of this contemporary verse translation.

Scene 1: Prologue and start of the action

During the contest in Aristophanes' comedy *Frogs* between 'Aeschylus' and 'Euripides' in Hades, Euripides is mocked because he claims that

> from the first words I gave everyone
> something to do; the wives had speeches, even slaves,
> masters, and girls, old women.
>
> (948–50 trans. Ewans 2010: 200)

He might have had *Medea* especially in mind; here two slaves (the first, what is more, an old woman) begin the play – and a wife will dominate its action.[2] Since the plot of *Medea* begins after a considerable back-story, the Nurse delivers the expository prologue, which is one of Euripides' standard dramatic techniques; the Tutor then enters to give more bad news – and he brings the two children with him, whose appearances onstage become increasingly more important as the drama unfolds. (Suspense is gradually increased; when will they enter the house for the last time?). Here they are already warned to keep away from their mother (100ff.).

But the radical dramaturgy of this scene does not end with the use of slaves and children. Starting at 96, Medea herself is heard crying out in despairing lyrics from inside the house, to which the Nurse responds. The Nurse is soon joined in the playing space (131) by the Women of Corinth, and unlike the usual uninterrupted entrance song, this play's Choros 1 is a *kommos* (a lyric lamentation), in dialogue with the Nurse's responses and disrupted by Medea's increasingly agitated outcries from within. In these ways the opening sequence of *Medea* (both Scene 1 and Choros 1) must have struck the Athenian audience as unusual and – as far as we can tell from the limited number of tragedies that survive to us – it is highly original. The effect is to heighten the interest in, sympathy for and focus on Medea when she finally appears before the Women in Scene 2.

We raised the house lights for some passages in *Medea* which can be played to address the audience directly. The aim was to break down the 'fourth wall' and make the audience feel that they were a community sharing in the drama (like the ancient Athenians in broad daylight), rather than just watching *Medea* as isolated individuals kept apart from each other and from the play by being in darkness. This device was used here in the Nurse's opening exposition (from 6 to 45), during the 'sufferings of women' section of Medea's big speech at the opening of Scene 2 (230–51) and for the Messenger from 1167 to the end of his speech. Audience address was also employed by the Women, in their Choral Interlude at 1081ff. and in the five lines which conclude the play; they advanced to the front of the stage, spread out in a line and spoke directly to the spectators.

The Nurse's prologue can begin as soon as she enters upstage, from the house, but in keeping with her address to the audience, she needs to come to the front of the stage, and subsequently move in that area, by line 6 ('Medea then,/my mistress . . .' – the point at which we raised the house lights). We felt that she is clearly not just the sons' nurse but also Medea's original nurse when she herself was a child, and has been brought with her mistress from Colchis. And so from 15 onward she must be passionate, deeply concerned by Jason's abandonment of Medea.

It should go without saying that real boys are needed in a production of *Medea*. (I cast two brothers aged 11 and 13, whose actions and expressions – and death-screams – were vital to the success of our performances). But two professional productions, one in Greece and one in Germany, dispensed with the sons; in the Greek one, the Tutor held up two white puppets, and in the German one, the children did not appear at all.³ Some amateur productions also omit the children. This destroys the whole emotional force of the play, in particular making nonsense of Medea's traumatic scene where the sight of her sons smiling at her overcomes for a few moments her resolve to kill them (Scene 6, 1021ff.).

The sons need to be occupied during the first part of the dialogue between the Nurse and the Tutor, during which they are ignored. In our production the boys entered with a soccer ball, which they tossed to and fro upstage, but when the Tutor told the Nurse that Creon intends to expel them and their mother from Corinth (69ff.), they stopped playing and approached the two adults at the front, listening intently from centre stage. This placed them in a good position for the Nurse to address them from right of front centre in 89ff. They obey her and go at the end of her speech towards the house, only to retreat when Medea is heard from inside it; since she cried out in lyrics in the original, in our production the music began at this point, intensifying the mood. Only after the Nurse's second speech to them, urging them to avoid going near Medea (98ff.), do the children and the Tutor enter the house. The Nurse's closing lines 122ff., addressed to the audience like the opening speech, stress the importance of moderation and the danger that Medea's outbursts presage.

Choros 1

Having the choros play ordinary people who are concerned about the welfare of a principal character is a convenient way of motivating their entrance; it is an approach that is found in other tragedies – for example, from this period, Sophocles' *Women of Trachis* and Euripides' *Hippolytus*. But in those two plays, the Women sing their entrance song uninterrupted; that is not the case in *Medea*, where the Women first interact with the Nurse, then are energized by a powerful outcry from Medea inside the house to burst into lyrics themselves with their first stanza (*strophe* A1, 148ff.). Interruptions resume as soon as their address to her is over (and Medea gives no sign in 160ff. that she has heard their lyrics); only when the Nurse has once again voiced her anxieties do they sing the corresponding *antistrophe* (A2, 174ff.). The Nurse agrees to the Women's request to ask Medea to come outside and meditates at 190ff. on the uselessness of music to heal grief, and on how it is superfluous at banquets (those of us who suffer from loud music making conversation impossible in restaurants, pubs and clubs may well agree with this sentiment from 2,452 years ago – though it hardly seems relevant to the situation at this point in the play); then she finally goes in to ask Medea to come outside. A few words from one of the Women to the others then prepare for Medea's entrance.

In most productions of Greek tragedy, the choros enters as a solemn phalanx, one immediately after another. We experimented for *Medea* with an alternative, which worked; each choros member entered only on her own lines, gradually building up to all four. This imparted an energy and dynamism to Choros 1, as well as solving the problem of having a group of people come onstage together and mostly stand silent (or worse still, declaim in unison). As this Choros has much of the quality of a dialogue scene, we decided not to give it formal patterned movement, even though all subsequent choral odes were treated in that way. Each actress simply entered in turn, speaking her lines, and they gathered around the Nurse – who then broke free and advanced to the front of the stage for her meditation at 190ff. In a naturalistic detail, the fourth and last Woman to enter tried to speak to the Nurse (205ff.), but the Nurse had already started to leave, so after her attempt to address her, the fourth Woman had to turn to her fellow members of the choros to complete the speech. This is an example of the sort of small touch, unthinkable for a production in a large arena theatre like Epidaurus or Delphi, that is effective in an intimate venue.

Scene 2 a: Medea addresses the women of Corinth

Unexpectedly, Medea comes out from the house and addresses the Women in calm, measured spoken words (she will not use lyric verse again). Her objective is to get them onto her side and to make them agree to stay silent as they witness the unfolding of her revenge on Jason. But she approaches this aim obliquely; first, she mentions the risk that she – especially as a foreigner – may be judged to be haughty. Next, she speaks, with her only reference back to her outcries in Scene 1 and Choros 1, of how her sufferings make her want to die. But then she changes direction again, and in famous lines criticizes the lot of women in the ancient world (which, indeed, has not been significantly changed in many places in the modern world). Finally, she emphasizes her isolation as an exile, falsely claiming that Jason abducted her from Colchis (255) but rightly stressing that she has no one to support her. With all this build-up, she finally asks the Women to be silent if she can find some means to revenge herself on Jason.

This speech plays well on a small stage with four Women seated at the front on opposite sides, facing Medea. She then has three audiences to which to turn: the two women in front of her on her left, the two on her right – and the public audience itself, directly in front of her. She can use all three – addressing the Women, alternating between those on her left and right, in the opening beat to 224; the women again at 225ff., but perhaps facing straight ahead in view of the greater passion of these lines; and then, advancing to the front of the stage, she can address the memorable words of 230ff. on the wretched lot of women, which the suffragettes recited at their rallies, to the actual audience in the theatre (we raised the house lights during this section). Then she needs to retreat up to centre stage so as to re-engage with the Women for her plea at 252ff. This final section of the speech draws to a fierce conclusion from 263 to 266, in which the actress can give a foretaste of the vengeful Medea to come.

One of the Women vows that they will keep silent because 'it's just for you to punish your husband, Medea' (267). They keep this promise, and after the deaths of Creon and the princess, they affirm that Jason has deserved his punishment (1231–2), again using the word 'justly'. But their complicity will be sorely stretched when Medea plans and subsequently executes the murder of her own children.

Scene 2 b: Medea and Creon (269ff.)

Creon enters the playing space left, from downtown Corinth. So far in Scene 2 this space outside the house, which is basically public, has become almost private as Medea has spoken to her friends about private matters – indeed, the Women have come as close as they can to Medea's own space indoors. Now it becomes a very public place as the king issues his orders.

Creon receives only a perfunctory announcement from one of the Women, which shows no deference to their king. Clearly, they are taking their role as Medea's supporters more seriously than their position as Corinthians. The ensuing scene is a direct clash between the objectives of the two solo characters. The audience already knows – but Medea does not – that Creon intends to expel her from Corinth; when told this, Medea realizes at once that it will not only disrupt her plans for revenge but is also virtually a death sentence, as she has literally nowhere to go. Medea shows that she can respond quickly to a new and disastrous situation; she has at the very least to mitigate his sentence of exile, and she has to do it right now. Her response is first to give an extended speech defending herself and assuring Creon (as we will soon discover, falsely) that she means him and his daughter no harm, and then to supplicate him, taking his hand and begging to stay for just one day. Creon admits that he is not really as harsh as a tyrant should be and yields to this request; his exit line is, ironically, 'You won't do any of the ghastly things I fear' (356).

We did not have soldiers accompanying Creon. On a small stage, a good actor can make his opening proclamation sufficiently menacing in itself – especially if he himself is wearing a military uniform, resplendent with a sash and medals, as he was in our production, as he advances toward Medea. She breaks away – and forward – in her initial despair (277ff.) before returning upstage to confront him. Her ensuing big speech (292ff.) plays well with the two characters mostly opposing each other halfway upstage.

The ensuing dialogue raises an important performance issue; when does Medea kneel and clasp Creon's hand? The choice is between 324 ('Don't do this, by your knees and the new bride') and 336 ('Don't do that, I beg you, Creon'). As the stage directions in the translation show, I opted for 336; Medea would be on the floor for too long if she knelt at 324, and there are opportunities for purposeful movement in the 1–1 line dialogue at 325ff. (e.g. for Medea to turn away forwards from Creon for 328–34), which makes it desirable for her to still be on her feet during this section. So at 324, she simply moved towards Creon, extending her hands in supplication.

A smile of joy is appropriate for Medea, in the light of her great relief when Creon tells her at 350 that she will get her wish before he withdraws his hand abruptly for his final warning. After he has gone, Medea, still on the ground, is comforted at 358ff. by one of the Women, who gently helps her to her feet. And Medea can address the opening two lines of the next section directly to this one woman. This is another example of how Euripides' play can be adapted to the intimacy expected and required on a small modern stage.

Scene 2 c: Medea contemplates her revenge (358ff.)

Left alone with the Women of Corinth, Medea reveals to them just how far she had to abase herself to deceive Creon into letting her stay for one more day; then she turns to how she will achieve her revenge, rejecting as impractical all alternatives except poison. But next she poses the question which will not be even partially resolved until the Aegeus scene; how can she herself survive after the killings? Finally, however, she summons up the courage to do the deed anyway; adopting Greek *male* values she states that she 'cannot be made a laughingstock / by Jason's marriage to a descendant of Sisyphus' (404–5), as she herself is of nobler ancestry.

Once again, as with Medea's first long speech, the key to making this one work in the end-on theatre is to vary the people to whom it is addressed. In our production the first two lines were spoken to the Woman who has helped her to her feet; then Medea delivered her next few lines alternately to the two groups of Women, before pacing to and fro sideways upstage during 376ff., where she is in doubt how she should kill her enemies. Then the invocation of Hekatē (395ff.) can be directed straight out towards the audience. And similarly, the self-exhortation at 401ff. plays well facing the audience, perhaps after a half-circle to bring Medea further upstage on the first two lines since the rest of the speech will be delivered with even more power and highly emotional gestures. On the last two lines, she should again move to include both groups of Women (who have remained seated during this speech and do not respond actively to it) in her generalization about their sex.

Choros 2

This Choros, like all of those to follow in this play, is divided between two A and two B stanzas. The A stanzas celebrate what the Women see as the imminence of recognition for women's abilities; the B stanzas turn to Medea's predicament, now that there is no respect for oaths.

In our production, Medea went into the house at the end of Scene 2. This was a difficult decision, but on a small stage, a lead character who is doing nothing would pull focus badly from the Women's words and movement during Choros 2, even if she were standing motionless upstage. Admittedly the Women address Medea in the B stanzas, but address to a person who is not onstage occurs several times in the surviving Greek tragedies, and especially in *Medea*.[4]

The mood to be aimed for in the music and movement is straightforward: joyful in the first two stanzas, sad in the second two. In all the Choroses in our production, the four Women moved, sometimes in unison, sometimes with the one person who was speaking performing individual movements of her own, and the movement director devised gestures and postures which illuminated the text.

Scene 3: Medea and Jason (1)

Medea comes out of the house simultaneously with the arrival of Jason from the palace downtown. In this scene he comes to offer support to Medea in her exile, but he enters unannounced and does not address her by name. Indeed, his opening remarks are supercilious, and they provoke a scathing attack from Medea – designed, as she says, both to 'lighten her soul' and to cause him pain as he hears (473–4). This turns the scene into a formal *agōn* (contest), which for the Athenian audience would have echoed the speeches for the prosecution and defence in a court of law, or those of men proposing opposing views on a motion in the Assembly.

Medea's speech, which would have been 'unwomanly' to Greek male ears both in its length and in her fierce intelligence, is followed by the conventional two-line punctuation of a comment from one of the Women, and then Jason launches into a shorter but equally argumentative response, after which one of the Women delivers their verdict. (In Greek tragedy, the private is made public.) In this contest of words both Medea and Jason go right back to the start of their relationship; Medea stresses all the things that she did for Jason, and the oaths of fidelity that he swore to her before the gods; she then goes on to describe the desperate circumstances in which he has now left her. Jason, by contrast, ascribes his success in Colchis not to Medea herself but to the goddess Aphrodite, who made her fall in love with him; then he patronizingly tells Medea how fortunate she is that he brought her to Greece. Finally, he too returns to the present and argues that his new marriage is the best thing for her and for the children. There is a strong element of sophistry – a live issue at Athens in the 430s BCE and onwards – in his whole speech (as well as outright misogyny at the end, 573–5), and I believe that many of the audience were (and are) likely to agree with the closing verdict from one of the Women:

> Jason, you have embellished your speech well;
> but, even if I speak against what you believe,
> I think that in betraying your wife you have not been just.
>
> (576–8)

After that, the scene descends into an unresolved tit-for-tat, until Jason remembers why he came and offers Medea and the children support in exile (610ff.). Medea refuses his aid ('the gifts of a bad man can do great harm', 618) and sends him off on his way to make love to his new bride.

The key to staging this long scene lies in setting out a clear pattern of movement which expresses which, if either, of the two characters is dominant at particular moments. The director and actors must decide when they are directly addressing each other, and when they break away. So Jason could, for example, circle arrogantly around Medea from 458, returning to his starting position upstage left as he turns to consider her impact on the royal family (453). Medea can hear him out in silence, equally balanced with him at upstage right; Jason should then approach her as he makes his offer of help (460ff.).

Medea begins her speech of denunciation where she stands, directly facing Jason, but it is good for her to break out as she begins her narrative at 475 (we had her cross in front of Jason and come downstage to centre left) and only go back upstage to be nearer to Jason on 482 ('I brought to you the light of salvation'). She could break out again briefly for the three lines from 495 ('Oh, my right hand . . .') before coming back close to Jason at 499. A similar manoeuvre is appropriate at 508 ('Oh, you made me blessed . . .'), with a swift turn back halfway through the next line, ready to give Jason the full force of her irony on 'with a marvellous and faithful husband'. A clearer and more decisive break away from him, which as he is upstage slightly left of centre has to be down to front right, is necessary for the appeal to Zeus at 516–19.

One of the Women stands up and interjects; to make this work Jason addressed the first two lines of his next speech to her, after which she resumed her seat. Then he tries to dominate over Medea as he delivers his defence – turning around her on his opening lines and deliberately upstaging her at 529–31. Only when delivering his little lecture on the benefits to her of living in Greece at 536ff. does he turn away, and we had him first stride to upstage centre and then, for the last three lines about himself, go to upstage right (542–4).

The combatants are now far apart, but Jason might well feel it necessary to dominate over Medea from upstage of her at 551ff., moving away after 555, but then from 557 directly facing her. However, we had him move forward and address the audience from downstage right for his diatribe against women (569ff.). In our production both Medea and three of the four Women of Corinth endured this misogyny in stoic silence, but one of them rose from her seat to call Jason out for treating his wife unjustly (576–8).

Medea directed the first five lines of her response to that Woman, only turning and stepping towards Jason on 'Take you!' (584) – at which point the Woman resumed her seat. The debate now rapidly heats up – and once again our Jason came close to Medea, upstage of her and trying to dominate at 593ff. ('Know this . . .'). Medea broke away with her passionate riposte:

> May I never live a prosperous life that's painful,
> nor have a kind of wealth that wounds the heart.
>
> (598–9)

They should be very close for the brief but furious 1–1 exchange at 605ff., but Jason obviously turns away and draws back when he refuses to continue the argument (609). He makes his offers of help distant from Medea (centre left when she is centre), and at the end of the scene, we had him take up Medea's sarcastic order to return to his 'newly tamed girl' immediately, as indicated in the stage directions – so her last two lines are cast at his departing back, gaining in intensity with every word.

Once again in our production Medea then went into the house, to avoid pulling focus from the words, music and movement of the next Choros.

This might not be necessary on a bigger stage and with a larger choros, as Medea's presence would be less obvious.

Choros 3

This is another ode in four stanzas, which is divided into two sections. In the A stanzas the Women pray for exactly what is plainly not present in the play – a gentle coming of Aphrodite, which does not disrupt a stable relationship with lust for another. Then in the B stanzas they brood on the horror of exile, and the fate of Medea, before condemning people like Jason.

The music and movement must support the words here; they should be subdued in the first two stanzas and passionate in the second two.

Scene 4 a: Medea and Aegeus

This scene has been much discussed. Aegeus' appearance 'out of the blue' has upset literary critics from Aristotle onwards (*Poetics* 1461b 21);[5] however, the fifth-century Greek audience would have regarded his arrival in this place at this time as anything but fortuitous. He provides the one thing Medea needs – a safe refuge – and at exactly the right time, on the very day, when she would otherwise have to undertake a form of revenge which would involve losing her life. Kovacs (1993) was right to note that in Medea's very first words after Aegeus' departure (764) she hails 'Zeus, Justice of Zeus and radiance of the Sun' (bear in mind that her grandfather the Sun God was, like Zeus himself, a defender of sworn oaths); he argued that these gods have brought Aegeus to Corinth today so that Medea can complete her revenge on Jason and gain security afterwards. Aristotle wrote about tragedy from what is effectively a secular perspective (he never discusses the role of the gods), so he could not be expected to understand this.

Aegeus states emphatically that he will not help Medea to get to Athens, and Medea accepts this; but she does not mention the means that she will be using to escape from Corinth after the murders, as that would spoil the surprise of the *coup de théâtre* in the Finale.

Once again Medea needs to use persuasion – but this time, as earlier with the Women, on a friend. She explains her predicament to Aegeus, and he is disturbed by Jason's conduct. Then she formally supplicates him, and when she has succeeded in her supplication, she requires Aegeus to swear an oath that he will not hand her over to her enemies; this he gladly gives, as it will safeguard him as well. Clearly we are meant to contrast this oath-giving with that of Jason, who formally swore fidelity to Medea in Colchis and will suffer extreme consequences for breaking his oaths to her.

After their initial greetings, Aegeus and Medea engage in a 1–1 line exchange during which she asks why he went to Delphi and then why he is going onwards to Troezen. But after 697, where I have marked a pause in the text, Medea should turn away from him; her line, 'Well, may you have good fortune and get what you want', is there to point the contrast between the solidity of Aegeus' plan and her own helpless situation. He is sensitive enough to notice this and brings out the reasons for Medea's distress in the ensuing dialogue; then, when he understands what has happened, he makes clear that he does not approve of what Jason has done (707). This precipitates a formal supplication by Medea; in the gestures of the ritual, she touches Aegeus' beard and knees, and begs him to give her refuge (709ff.). Aegeus, who is her friend, does not refuse this supplication; he should raise Medea to her feet on 719 – but then releases her hands and moves away on 723, as he embarks on telling her that she must make her own way to Athens. Medea accepts this and demands that he must swear an oath to keep her safe when she has come to his city; much should be made of this solemn oath, with Medea raising her hands to the heavens on 746–7 and Aegeus mirroring her gesture as he formally swears at 752–3.

The scene then ends as abruptly as it began; our Aegeus took Medea's hand on 755 to show that his oath is binding, and she then withdrew hers on 'and so farewell'. In our production Claudia Bedford as Medea, after turning away from her Aegeus, put considerable feeling into 'and have got what I want' (758), prefiguring what is to come after Aegeus departs, sent on his way by good wishes from one of the Women. This scene plays perfectly on an intimate stage.

Scene 4 b: Medea's plan

Medea exults in now having a safe haven in Athens. Then she reveals her plan to the Women; she will lure Jason into thinking that she has reconsidered and approves of his new marriage; then she will send her sons with poisoned presents to the royal bride. But now she reveals that she will have to kill her children: 'It's not tolerable, friends, if enemies can laugh at you' (797). And only in this way can she fully punish Jason. The Women protest vigorously, but Medea is implacable.

An Attendant must enter from the house immediately after Aegeus leaves, since she is needed to take the message to Jason at the end of the scene. It is probable that in Euripides' original production two attendants entered with Medea on her first appearance at 214, but extras upstage pull focus in a small proscenium arch theatre, so it is best for the Attendant (on a small stage we only require one) to appear only at this point when she will be needed. This involves altering 950–1 from 'Let one of my Attendants bring this finery . . .' to 'Attendant, bring this finery'.

Medea now once again dominates centre stage and should alternate her delivery between the two groups of Women. When she tells them, 'I have to kill my children' (792), our entire choros stood up abruptly and advanced upstage towards Medea, who threw out her hands in fury to stop them coming close and then proceeded to outline the rest of her plan. When she had finished, one of the Women courageously approached her to object, taking Medea' hand; Medea rejects the hand savagely and answers with equal intensity the next two Women who approach her to speak before going upstage to instruct the Attendant. Then she exits without another word.

Choros 4

Medea leaves the playing space and goes indoors to anoint the robe and crown with poisons. (This is essential – the Greek theatre was realistic in such matters,[6] and there is no problem in the Women addressing Medea in her absence in the B stanzas).[7] The first two stanzas glorify Athens; then in B1 the Women ask how such a city can receive the murderess of her own children, and in B2 they wonder where she can get the daring for such a dreadful deed. Accordingly, the music and movement for the first two stanzas should be lyrical and beautiful respectively, with a sharp contrast for the sheer horror that is developed in the remainder of the ode. We used lights on the fingers of the Women to create an effect here; each moved her hands and arms in patterns while her lights were lit during her stanza and then passed her stanza to the next as if throwing a ball; her lights were then extinguished as those of the next speaker, catching the imaginary ball, went on. The contrast was great between the blue lights of the first two speakers and the red lights of the last two.

Scene 5: Medea and Jason (2)

Medea's speech is a masterpiece of deception; an actress here plays the part of a character who reveals herself as a brilliant actress. Medea even imagines herself attendant on Jason's new marriage-bed, in the role normally played by the mother of the bride! (Claudia Bedford allowed herself a slightly bitter tone on 'your bride', 888, as if fantasizing this extreme idea is almost too much for Medea.) Jason's naivety and complacency are shown by the fact that he wholly accepts her 'apology'. Even though the presence of the children whom she is about to kill causes Medea to weep twice (900ff., 922ff.), she manages to explain this away to Jason in a way that he believes. Finally, she persuades him without much difficulty to let the boys take her gifts of robe and crown to the princess on the pretext (which works, cf. 1002–3) that the gifts will persuade the bride to let Jason's sons stay in Corinth.

This scene needs careful blocking. There should be plenty of movement in the first speech, with much of it before 884 directed inwards, away from Jason. Then when the boys come in, the Tutor and the Attendant need to stand directly in front of the house façade, while the boys advance only about one-third downstage and on the left; this is so that Medea has space to turn away downstage right when she is weeping – and after Jason's speech to the boys at 914ff. he can detach and cross over to Medea on 922ff. The ensuing dialogue between Medea and Jason can be played across the front of the stage, except of course that Medea turns upstage to give orders to the Attendant.

We made the unusual decision to take Jason off after 968. ('I'd give not just gold but my life'.) He strode off, yielding ungraciously to Medea's appeal to him, and left the children behind with Medea to receive her instructions. After that they departed stage left with the Tutor, taking the gifts, and the Attendant went into the house. In our production, the boys started to leave fast on 'Go quickly', 974, and Medea knelt centre stage as she completed her speech, exhausted by what she has done.

Choros 5

Once again, a Choros is divided between its two pairs of stanzas. In A1–2 the Women contemplate the fate of the children and the imminent death of the princess-bride; in the B stanzas they first condemn Jason and then pity Medea.

This is a grim and miserable ode throughout (Euripides uses the word 'unfortunate' three times in four stanzas!). The mood does not change, but it intensifies in the last two stanzas. I assigned the last stanza, addressed to Medea, to the Woman who had sympathized with Medea at 358ff. and condemned Jason at 576ff., so establishing her character as more sympathetic to Medea than the other Women. Differentiating the individual characters of the choros members is both possible and desirable in an intimate theatre with a small choros.

Scene 6: Medea and her sons

In this extraordinary and powerful scene, Medea, after a few words with the Tutor, is left alone with her sons for the first time in the play. Her misery is so great that for a few moments she considers abandoning her plans (1040–8), but she steels herself and then brings the children close to her, hugging them, aware that this will be for the last time. After they have left, she acknowledges how great a crime she will commit, but 'anger has control over my plans' (1079).

This is one of the most demanding scenes for an actress in extant Greek tragedy. The Greek text is corrupt (for the decisions made in this translation, see 'Translation Notes'), but once a viable performance text is agreed upon, all that matters is to convey Medea's terrible, raw and changing emotions, now that the events which she has set in motion have stripped from her all the deceit and cunning that she has had to adopt in earlier scenes. Until 1026 she should address her sons directly, in a gradual build to 1039. After that, the smiles on the children's faces are too much for her, and she retreats upstage and turns away from them. A turn towards two of the Women, then back to the children on 'as I look on the bright eyes of my sons' (1043), motivates her decision to abandon her plans. The following few lines, in which she decides not to murder them, are best played moving to and fro upstage. But the return to her resolve needs to be played out to the audience (1049–66). Then in a burst of emotion she goes to her children, takes their hands and hugs them for one last time (1067–75). Finally, this overwhelms her, and she abruptly sends them off into the house. Her last three lines can be directed to the Women and to the audience.

Choral interlude

The Women outline 'normal parental worries', in pointed contrast with how Medea will treat her children.[8] But these normal parental worries conclude with the early deaths of children (infant and child mortality rates were high in the ancient world), so there is obvious relevance to what is happening in the play.

This Interlude profits greatly from division at every full stop between different members of the choros so that each successive Woman picks up on the previous one's contribution and takes it further. In our production the Women advanced to the front of the stage and addressed their comments partially to each other but primarily directly to the audience; as with previous sections of audience address, the house lights were up for this Interlude. A percussive beat in the soundtrack differentiated the Interlude from previous choral odes, and a turning point was marked at 1098 ('But as for those who have the joy/of children in their house . . .'); the actress spoke the word 'joy' as if in inverted commas, questioning whether having children really is a joy; then the intensity of both the music and the delivery of the text increased steadily from this point to the anguished question voiced by the last speaker (1112–15).

Scene 7: The deaths of the princess and of Creon

Prior to the development of effective illusion in film, violent and horrific action could only be realistically conveyed to an audience by means of narrative – a medium at which the Greeks had excelled from the Homeric poems onwards. All Athenians, both male and female, had far more exposure to the violence endemic in human life than most inhabitants of first-world countries today. Every male from the age of 18 fought regularly, often each year, hand to hand to defend his city-state; every female from soon after the time of first menstruation became initiated into the realities of childbearing in a society where medicine was primitive by modern western standards. So the ancient Greeks saw far more bloodshed and human suffering than most modern westerners do; it is therefore no surprise that the Homeric epics, the vase-paintings and friezes and the messenger speeches in tragedy depict violence objectively and realistically.

This long but superbly paced messenger speech is at a very high level of vividness, detail and intensity. It prepares for the final phases of the play – the murder of the children and the concluding confrontation between Medea and Jason. It is initially directed to Medea, and the Messenger must maintain some contact with her, but most of it plays best directly to the audience; accordingly, we raised the house lights from 1167 to the end of the speech.

The speech requires a virtuoso performance. The actor must not only provide a gripping narrative but must use gestures and body posture to help to re-create in the spectators' minds the actions of the characters in the story, and also impersonate their voices where there is direct quotation of their actual words.

Two student productions preserved on YouTube had actors miming the parts of the princess and Creon during the climactic section of the messenger speech.[9] The problem with this is that the depiction of the poisons' gradual disfigurement of the girl, and the death of Creon, cannot be mimed on stage with any credibility sufficient to match the words; indeed only a movie studio using computer-generated effects would be able to represent visually the full horror of what the Messenger recounts.

A modern Medea, acting without a mask in a far smaller theatre than Euripides', needs to support the Messenger by demonstrating her initial joy at the news of the deaths and then her increasing exultation as the gruesome narrative unfolds. Next, after the exit of the Messenger comes the Women's verdict on Jason, that his sufferings are just – and then Medea launches into her heart-wrenching final speech before murdering her children (1236ff.). Here we deployed a lighting effect; see the following section.

Choros 6: The murder of the children

This is the last and most dramatic example in *Medea* of division of a four-stanza ode at the midpoint. In the original Greek text, Euripides used, for the first time in this play, the dochmiac – the lyric metre of the utmost excitement. Medea has gone into the house; the Women pray frantically for the Sun God to hold her back (A1) and warn of the terrible consequences of kindred murder (A2). Then a boy's cry for help is heard from inside the house, and the B1 stanza extraordinarily incorporates spoken dialogue between the sons, and their futile call for the Women to help them, before all is over. In B2 the Women recall Ino, the one parallel that they can think of (though other women in Greek legend, especially Procne, could come to mind as well); it is as if this stanza is there to refute in advance Jason's claim in the Finale that 'no Greek woman would have dared to do this' (1339).

No good production of this play is complete without drastic effects for the moments before, during and immediately after the murder of the children. We cross-faded the lights to flood the stage in red part way through Medea's final speech before going in (beginning at 'Arm yourself, my heart . . .', 1242), and after an intense build-up in the music and in the declamation of the Women (some of them in shadow, others in red light) during the first two stanzas of Choros 6, we halted the music – an effect designed to shock, as it had never been done in a previous Choros. The stanza during which the sons call out and are then murdered was spoken (and screamed!) unaccompanied. During this stanza the Women reacted in horror, two of them approaching the doors – but too late, as the second death-cry sounded just before they reached the entrance. Music only returned, in a very sombre and reflective mood, during the Ino-stanza which concludes the Choros (1283ff.), and white light was only restored when Jason entered after that for the Finale.

The Women must of course remain standing after this Choros, ready for their exchanges with Jason.

Scene 8 (finale): Medea and Jason (3)

After death-cries from within, the Athenian audience would at the end of Choros 6 have expected the *ekkuklēma* (rolling-out machine) to emerge from the doors of the house, with a tableau of the bodies of the dead children and perhaps Medea defending her deed over them like Clytemnestra in Aeschylus' *Agamemnon* (1373ff.), but instead, in a tremendous *coup de théâtre*, Euripides used the *mēchanē* to elevate Medea's triumph to a whole new level, both literally and metaphorically – while also solving the as yet unresolved question of how she is to escape from Corinth to Athens.

When Jason appears at the start of the scene, the red lights cross-fade rapidly back to white. The intimacy of the playing space allowed for one of the Women to approach Jason on 1306–7 and for another to take his hand tentatively as she delivers the dreadful truth (1309): 'Your children are dead, slain by their own mother'. The fourth Woman to speak invites Jason to open the doors, and he batters on them – creating for the Greek audience the expectation that a tableau will emerge on the *ekkuklēma*, but then Medea enters on high. At once we reduced the lighting to the spotlights on Medea and Jason; the Women retreated to as far away as possible from Medea, standing in darkness against the left wall. They take no further part in the action, speaking only when it is all over.

Although she is a mortal woman, and argues with Jason as such, Medea here possesses some of the characteristics of the gods, demigods and goddesses who appear on the crane (*mēchanē*) at the end of later plays of Euripides and in Sophocles' *Philoctetes*; she imposes her will, founds a cult and prophesies the future. Critics are divided about this final appearance of Medea; for one commentator, 'Because the play has avoided giving Medea supernatural powers before the murders her transformation into something like a god after them is chilling . . . [the sacrifice of the children] makes her both less and more than human'.[10] Others have gone further:

> She has forfeited her humanity by her tragic choice. In fact she has become utterly inhuman in her gloating over Jason's loss [here the author quotes 1396: 'You are not really mourning yet; wait for old age'] and for the first time there is pity for him as well, who in his human grief and powerlessness acquires a certain stature, a tragic dignity which he did not have before.[11]

By contrast Swift argues:

> Medea's godlike behavior in the final scene should not be regarded as a complete transformation, for her new supernatural powers do not completely efface the human aspects of her personality. She continues to be drawn into bitter argument with Jason, and her passionate hatred of him is unlike the calm and detached attitudes of Euripidean gods. Whereas human characters have no choice but to accept the edicts of the gods, Jason continues to treat Medea as his wife, and to curse and call down divine justice upon her.[12]

As with many scholarly disagreements about Greek plays, the resolution of this one depends almost entirely on how the scene is performed; it is the responsibility of the director and actors. In the original performance, Medea was on high and in her golden chariot; Jason is left to confront her from below in the *orchēstra*. Those immutable facts determine their relative power positions, but how Medea is to be viewed – as human, inhuman, semi-divine or a mixture of all these elements – depends on how her lines are played. And similarly, the question of whether the audience is now to feel any pity or sympathy for Jason depends on how the scene as a whole is performed.

Our theatre had no fly tower, so an appearance of Medea *ex machina* in an airborne golden chariot was not possible (nor would it have been desirable in the intimate terms of this production). Instead, we made use of a platform and a lighting and costume change to achieve an appropriate effect; Medea appeared upstage right on a platform raised one metre above the playing space, in a golden spotlight and wearing a gleaming, almost goddess-like gold and black striped dress, a tiara and high-heeled sandals; all of this allowed the actress to emphasize Medea's absolute authority over Jason, who stood – and subsequently kneeled – in another, blue spotlight upstage centre. There was no other lighting after Medea's appearance, so the separation between them was marked.

In our production, after experimenting with different ways of performing the text, we chose to make Medea absolutely cold and heartless – for example, taunting Jason openly, almost sarcastically on 1399: 'Yes, to cause you pain'. She has done the deed; she has her revenge. And Jason's grief was heartfelt; he knelt in agony at 1346–1360, where he contemplates the disasters that have befallen him and suffers Medea's implacable response, and we made a big moment of his final speech after Medea has left. It was again spoken on his knees, beginning with an immense outcry to Zeus and ending in incoherent weeping. In this way, we tried to generate some sympathy for Jason, to offset the poor figure which he cut earlier, and the fact that he has received his just deserts – but four lives have been horrifically lost, two of them innocent children. I feel that the audience should be totally disturbed by the end of *Medea*, quite unable to evaluate right and wrong in the terrible outcome which they have witnessed.

After Jason collapsed in tears, the lights cross-faded and the Women advanced to the front of the stage. They delivered the last words unaccompanied, one line for each of the four; then the final line, 'That's how this story ends', was the one and only unison speech in the entire production – followed instantly by a blackout.[13]

Notes

1 Ewans (forthcoming).
2 Aeschylus' *Agamemnon* begins with a monologue by one slave, the Watchman, but Euripides' use of two slaves in this opening scene is unique in extant tragedy.

Not however in comedy; Aristophanes has two slaves initiating the action in both *Knights* and *Peace*.

3 National Theatre of Greece 1998; Schauspiel Frankfurt 2013. Details in Ewans forthcoming, appendix.

4 Cf. e.g. Aeschylus, *Agamemnon* 83ff. with note at Ewans 1995: 132 supporting Taplin 1977: 280–5. There are examples elsewhere of choral address to an absent character; Euripides *Hippolytus* 141–69, Sophocles *Aias* 134–200 and *Antigone* 944–87 (Mossman 2011: 297). In *Medea* stanzas in every Choros are addressed to Medea, who is certainly offstage during Choroses 1, 4 and 6 (see further commentary below).

5 If indeed Aristotle's reference is to *Medea* and not to something that happened in Euripides' lost tragedy *Aegeus*. But that is unlikely.

6 So rightly Mossman 2011: 296–7 against Mastronade 2002: 204.

7 See note 4.

8 McDermott 1989: 63.

9 These and other productions of *Medea* are discussed in the appendix to Ewans (forthcoming).

10 Scodel (2010: 131).

11 March 1990: 43. Cf. Cunningham 1954: 159.

12 Swift 2016: 16–17.

13 I have no doubt that the closing lines are genuine, despite the occurrence of similar (but not identical) lines at the end of other tragedies by Euripides. Cf. 'Translation Notes', p. 59.

Cast and production team

The first performance of this translation was by Stray Dogs Theatre Company in the Newcastle Theatre Company Theatre in Lambton, New South Wales on 12 May 2021.

CAST (in order of appearance)

NURSE	Carol Hong
TUTOR	Ian Robinson
MEDEA'S SONS	Sam and Noah Lane
WOMEN OF CORINTH	Aimee Cavanagh
	Emma Crowther
	Tracey Gordon
	Melody Thorburn
MEDEA	Claudia Bedford
CREON, KING OF CORINTH	Ian Robinson
JASON	Phillip Ross
AEGEUS, KING OF ATHENS	Richard Murray
ATTENDANT	Hannah Richens
MESSENGER	Derek Fisher

PRODUCTION TEAM

TRANSLATOR/DIRECTOR	Michael Ewans
ASSISTANT DIRECTOR/ CHORAL MOVEMENT	Jessica Alexander-Lillicrap
DRAMATURG	Marguerite Johnson
STAGE MANAGER	Jane Cobley
COMPOSER	Simon Ritchie
SET	David Murray
COSTUME DESIGNER	Melinda Hicks
LIGHTING DESIGNER	Sophie Botta

Glossary of names

Aegeus   King of Athens.

Aietes   King of Colchis, father of Medea.

Aphrodite   Goddess of love.

Apollo   God of prophecy; oracles were given at his temple in Delphi.

Argo   The ship in which Jason and the other Argonauts went to Colchis to retrieve the Golden Fleece (q.v.).

Bosporus   The narrow strait at the eastern end of the Propontis (modern Sea of Marmara), leading into the Black Sea.

Cēphisus   The principal river flowing near Athens, to the west.

Clashing Rocks   Two rocks which clashed together from opposite sides of the Bosporus to destroy ships. The Argonauts used a trick (sending a dove ahead and then rowing hard through the gap while the rocks were returning to their respective shores) to enable them to pass through safely.

Colchis   A kingdom on the east coast of the Black Sea, in modern Georgia.

Corinth   The city on the Isthmus which joins the Peloponnese to the northern Greek mainland. At the time when this play was performed, tensions between Athens and Corinth were rising, and they led the next month to the start of the Peloponnesian War.

Creon   King of Corinth in this play. His name means 'ruler'.

Eros   Son of Aphrodite, capable of exciting sexual passion by shooting invisible arrows from his golden bow at mortals.

Golden Fleece   Nephelē saved her two children, Phrixos and Hellē, from the wrath of Athamas' second wife, Ino, by enabling them to escape on a flying golden ram. Hellē fell off and drowned (the Hellespont [Dardanelles] was named after her), but Phrixos managed to reach Colchis, where the king Aietes received him kindly and gave him one of his daughters, Chalciopē, in marriage. Aietes sacrificed the ram to Zeus and hung the Fleece in a grove where a serpent guarded it.

Hades   Name both of the underworld and of its king.

Hekatē A goddess of the underworld, queen of the ghosts and goddess of magic.

Hera Wife of Zeus and Queen of the gods. Her cult as Hera Acraia was based in her temple near Perachora, 32 kilometres north of Corinth.

Hermes The messenger-god also safeguarded travellers on the dangerous roads of ancient Greece.

Ino She nursed the god Dionysus, Zeus' son by the mortal woman Semelē. Hera was angry with her for this. There are various versions of when and how she was driven mad; in this play it seems that the madness was inflicted by Hera, and Ino killed both herself and her two sons (Euripides thereby suggests a parallel with Medea). She was transformed into a minor goddess, Leucothea.

Iolcus Capital of Thessaly, the main kingdom of northern Greece. Modern Volos.

Jason Son of Aison. See 'Backstory', p. 18.

Medea One of the daughters of Aietes, king of Colchis. See 'Backstory' (p. 18), and 'Aftermath' (p. 56).

Olympus A high mountain in northern Greece, believed to be the residence of the gods.

Orpheus A legendary musician, son of one of the Muses and husband (all too briefly) of Eurydice. His love for his wife contrasts strongly with Jason's abandonment of Medea.

Pan A rustic god, often imaged with the horns, ears and legs of a goat. One of his powers is to create 'panic' – wild, groundless fear.

Pandion An early king of Athens, in this play the father of Aegeus.

Peirēnē A well-known spring in Corinth.

Pelias Usurper of the throne of Thessaly by deposing Aison; he lived in fear of the 'one-sandaled man' who it was prophesied would supersede him. When Pelias' young nephew Jason, who was raised by Cheiron the centaur because Jason's mother did not trust Pelias, arrived at court wearing only one sandal, Pelias sent him on the expedition to retrieve the Golden Fleece. For what happened to Pelias when Jason returned to Greece with Medea, see 'Backstory' (p. 18).

Pēlion A mountain in Magnesia (part of the kingdom of Thessaly), overlooking Iolcus.

Pelops Son of Tantalus, founder of the kingdom of Argos/Mycenae. He had many children, including Pittheus.

Pieria The district in northern Greece which surrounded Mt. Olympus (q.v.).

Pittheus King of Troezen. When Aegeus arrived there, Pittheus easily interpreted the oracle, got Aegeus drunk and induced Aegeus to sleep with his daughter Aethra. Their son was Theseus, later to become Athens' greatest hero.

Procne   Sister of Philomela, who was raped by Procne's husband Tereus; he cut out her tongue so she could not divulge the rape. But she embroidered it and sent the needlework to her sister; in revenge, Procne killed her own son Itys and served him up at a banquet to his father. Tereus sought to kill the two women, but he was transformed into a hoopoe, Procne into a nightingale and Philomela into a swallow.

Sisyphus   The infamous founder of the royal house of Corinth; a trickster who was punished in Hades by being forced endlessly to push a giant stone up a hill, after which it would roll down, and he had to push it up again.

Scylla   Once a beautiful girl, transformed by a jealous rival into a monster with six dog heads, which could seize and devour mariners as they sailed past her cave (traditionally in the Straits of Messina, hence 'Etruscan').

Sun, The   (Hēlios) A god, who among his other powers was a guardian of sworn oaths.

Themis   A goddess whose name means 'law'; she was the mother of Justice and of the Fates.

Troezen   City in Epidauria, some distance southeast of Corinth.

Zeus   The chief god, and very important in this play because of his role as the defender of sworn oaths, who punished those who broke them.

Bibliography

Adkins, A.W.H. (1960) *Merit and Responsibility: A Study in Greek Values*. Oxford: Clarendon Press.

Blondell, R. (trans.). (1999) 'Medea' in *Women on the Edge: Four Plays by Euripides* (eds. and trans. R. Blondell, M.-K. Gamel, N.S. Rabinowitz, and B. Zweig). New York: Routledge.

Bongie, E.B. (1977) 'Heroic Elements in the *Medea* of Euripides' *TAPA* 107, 27–56.

Cunningham, M.P. (1954) 'Medea ΑΠΟ ΜΗΧΑΝΗΣ' *Classical Philology* 49.3, 151–60.

Diggle, J. (ed.). (1984) *Euripides: Fabulae*, vol. 1. Oxford: Clarendon Press.

Easterling, P.E. (1977) 'The Infanticide in Euripides' *Medea*' *Yale Classical Studies* 25, 177–91.

Ewans, M. (ed. and trans.). (1995) *Aeschylus: Oresteia*. London: Everyman.

———. (ed. and trans.). (1996) *Aeschylus: Suppliants and Other Dramas*. London: Everyman.

———. (1999) *Sophocles: Four Dramas of Maturity* (ed. and trans., with Graham Ley and Gregory McCart). London: Everyman.

———. (2000) *Sophocles: Three Dramas of Old Age* (ed. and trans., with Graham Ley and Gregory McCart). London: Everyman.

———. (2007) *Opera from the Greek: Studies in the Poetics of Appropriation*. Aldershot: Ashgate (Reprint 2016 Abingdon and New York: Routledge).

———. (ed. and trans.). (2010) *Aristophanes: Lysistrata, the Women's Festival and Frogs*. Norman: Oklahoma University Press.

———. (ed. and trans.). (2011) *Aristophanes: Acharnians, Knights and Peace*. Norman: Oklahoma University Press.

———. (forthcoming) *Staging Greek Drama: A Practical Guide for Directors, Actors and Drama Students*.

Goldhill, S. (2007) *How to Stage Greek Tragedy Today*. Chicago: University of Chicago Press.

Hall, E. (2010) 'Medea and the Mind of the Murderer' in *Unbinding Medea: Interdisciplinary Approaches to a Classical Myth from Antiquity to the 21st Century* (eds. H. Bartel and A. Simon). Abingdon: Legenda, 16ff.

Hall, E., Macintosh, F., and Taplin, O. (eds.). (2001) *Medea in Performance 1500–2000*. Oxford: Legenda.

Johnston, S. (1997) 'Corinthian Medea and the Cult of Hera Akraia' in *Medea* (eds. J. Clauss and S. Johnston). Princeton: Princeton University Press, 44–70.

Knox, B. (1979) 'The *Medea* of Euripides' in *Word and Action: Essays on the Ancient Theater*. Baltimore: Johns Hopkins University Press, 295–322.

Kovacs, D. (1993) 'Zeus in Euripides' *Medea*' *American Journal of Philology* 114, 45–70.

Ley, G. (2006) *A Short Introduction to the Greek Theater*, 2nd ed. Chicago: Chicago University Press.

Ley, G. and Ewans, M. (1985) 'The *Orchestra* as Acting Area in Greek Tragedy' *Ramus* 14.2, 75–84.

Maravela-Solbakk, A. (2008) 'Euripides' *Medea* 723–30 Revisited' *Classical Quarterly* N.S. 58.2, 452–60.

March, J. (1990) 'Euripides the Misogynist?' in *Euripides, Women and Sexuality* (ed. A. Powell). London: Routledge.

Mastronade, D.J. (ed.). (2002) *Euripides: Medea*. Cambridge: Cambridge University Press.

McCart, G. (trans.). (1998) '*Medea* by Euripides' in *Word for Word* (ed. J. Senczuk). Wollongong: Five Islands Press.

McDermott, E. (1989) *Euripides' Medea: The Incarnation of Disorder*. University Park, PA: Pennsylvania State University Press.

Michelini, A.N. (1989) 'Neophron and Euripides' *Medeia* 1056–80' *TAPA* 119, 115–35.

Moorwood, J. (trans.). (2008) *Euripides Medea, Hippolytus, Electra and Helen*. Oxford: Oxford University Press.

Mossman, J. (ed.). (2011) *Euripides: Medea*. Oxford: Aris and Philips (Oxbow Books).

Olson, S.D. (ed.). (1988) *Aristophanes: Peace*. Oxford: Oxford University Press.

Page, D.L. (ed.). (1938) *Euripides: Medea*. Oxford: Oxford University Press.

Rayor, D.J. (trans.). (2013) *Euripides: Medea*. New York: Cambridge University Press.

Reeve, M. (1972) 'Euripides: *Medea* 1021–80' *Classical Quarterly* 22.1, 59–61.

Rehm, R. (1992) *Greek Tragic Theatre*. London: Routledge.

Scodel, R. (2010) *An Introduction to Greek Tragedy*. Cambridge: Cambridge University Press.

Seidensticker, B. (1990) 'Euripides *Medea* 1056–80, an Interpolation?' in *Cabinet of the Muses: Essays on Classical and Comparative Literature in Honor of Thomas G. Rosenmeyer* (eds. M. Griffith and D.J. Mastronarde). Atlanta: Scholars Press.

Stanford, W.B. (1983) *Greek Tragedy and the Emotions: An Introductory Study*. London: Routledge and Kegan Paul.

Steiner, G. (1975) *After Babel: Aspects of Language and Translation*. London: Oxford University Press.

Studdart, D. (ed. and trans.). (2014) *Looking at Medea*. London: Bloomsbury Academic.

Svarlien, D.A. (trans.). (2008) *Euripides: Medea*. Indianapolis: Hackett.

Swift, L. (2016) 'Medea' in *The Blackwell Companion to Euripides* (ed. L. McClure). Oxford: Blackwell.

Taplin, O. (1977) *The Stagecraft of Aeschylus: The Dramatic Use of Entrances and Exits in Greek Tragedy*. Oxford: Clarendon Press.

———— (trans.). (2013) *Euripides: Medea*. Chicago: Chicago University Press.

Thompson, E.A. (1944) 'Neophron and Euripides' *Medea*' *Classical Quarterly* 38.1–2, 10–14.

Wiles, D. (1997) *Tragedy in Athens: Performance Space and Theatrical Meaning*. Cambridge: Cambridge University Press.

Audiovisual resources

The dress rehearsal of the first production of this translation, on which the Theatrical Commentary is based, may be found on YouTube at https://youtu.be/B5No7E56zxE or by entering EURIPIDES MEDEA NEWCASTLE AUSTRALIA 2021. There are errors in this recorded performance, which were corrected before first night.

Entering EURIPIDES MEDEA will give access to other productions of the play; they are assessed in the Appendix to Ewans (forthcoming).

Index

Printed in the United States
by Baker & Taylor Publisher Services